Opportunity Road
Yonge Street 1860 to 1939

About the Author

Scottish-born F.R. "Hamish" Berchem sailed in submarines with the Royal Navy before transferring to the Royal Canadian Navy. He was Commanding Officer, HMCS *York*, Toronto, from 1970 to 1973, and has commanded vessels on the coast of Labrador, as well as HMCS *Porte Dauphine* and CSS *Bayfield*, both on the Great Lakes. Recently he sailed as Chief Officer and Master of Fisheries and Oceans. He has honours and masters degrees in history and English from the University of Toronto and has taught high school at Don Mills and Bathurst Heights Collegiates in North York. He is a skilled painter in watercolour and has had several one-man shows. He is also the author of *Ships in Bottles* (Stoddart), and *The Yonge Street Story 1793-1860* (Natural Heritage).

OPPORTUNITY ROAD

YONGE STREET 1860 TO 1939

F.R. BERCHEM

NATURAL HERITAGE / NATURAL HISTORY INC.

To Pat
Whose ideas encouraged this story.

Acknowledgments

The author would like to express his appreciation of the considerable help and advice that he received from Mrs. Patricia Hart of Richmond Hill Public Library. Also to the several historical societies and associations and archives which made their material so readily available.

Opportunity Road: Yonge Street 1860 to 1939
by F.R. Berchem

Published 1996 by Natural Heritage / Natural History Inc.
P.O. Box 95, Station "O", Toronto, Ontario M4A 2M8

Printed and bound in Canada by Hignell Printing Limited, Winnipeg, Manitoba
Designed by Robin Brass Studio

Canadian Cataloguing in Publication Data

Berchem, F.R., 1931—
Opportunity Road: Yonge Street 1860 to 1939

Includes bibliographical references and index.
ISBN 1-896219-15-2

1. Yonge Street (Toronto, Ont., – History. 2. Toronto (Ont.) – History. 3. Ontario – History – 1841-1867.* 4. Ontario – History – 1867-1918.* 5. Ontario – History – 1918-1945.* I. Title.

FC3097.67.B469 1996   971.3'54102   C96-931562-7
F1059.5.T6875Y65 1996

Natural Heritage / Natural History Inc. acknowledges with gratitude the assistance of The Canada Council, The Ontario Arts Council and The Association for the Export of Canadian Books.

CONTENTS

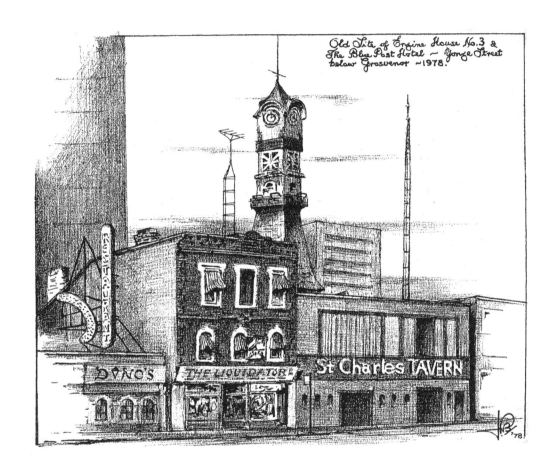

Old Site of Engine House No. 3 &
The Blue Post Hotel ~ Yonge Street
below Grosvenor ~1978.

RESTAURANT

DINO'S   THE LIQUIDATOR   St Charles TAVERN

INTRODUCTION

T.S. Eliot's words, "In my end is my beginning," best describe my interest in the history of Yonge Street. I began with Penetanguishene where "a safe and commodious Harbour" had been selected for military purposes. My curiosity about the motives behind such a choice led me to the volumes of correspondence of Upper Canada's first Lieutenant-Governor, John Graves Simcoe, into whose strategic designs it had fitted. This led in turn to the story of the development of Yonge Street itself.

The research absorbed much of my time during the 1970s and covered the period from 1791 to 1860. 1860 seemed to mark the logical end to the tale of the Street's establishment in history. By that time the military barracks at Penetanguishene had become a reformatory; the wars were over and the great political disputes played out; the great antagonists died, William Lyon Mackenzie in 1861 and Bishop Strachan in 1867. The railways were the harbingers of a new age in which Yonge Street would become just one more humdrum road; — or so I thought.

The extent to which my account of Yonge Street to 1860 was positively received and the curiosity which it aroused came as a pleasant surprise to me, as did the questions about the subsequent history of the Street. And so I was encouraged to continue my research until when my job took me to the East Coast. During that time, talks to various historical societies had brought out many local stories and from them came a realization that Yonge Street had indeed continued to be a vibrant pulse for the growing city. Opportunities for success had burgeoned along with Toronto's increasing importance, and particularly with the economic boost from the American Civil War.

The results from this would have amazed Simcoe. He had hoped to establish an aristocracy along English lines in Upper Canada. He had no great enthusiasm for businessmen and merchants, and would probably have looked askance at the emergence of an extremely successful class of grocers and shopkeepers, most of them Scots. Many of them had an association with Yonge Street after 1860, and they became a powerful force in the shaping of Upper Canadian society.

From my reading I have formed the opinion that a strong bond developed between business and the Methodist Church whose influence Bishop Strachan had vainly tried to constrain. The short-tempered, eccentric Tory Colonel Thomas

Talbot had roundly denounced all "Methodists, total abstainers and disloyal persons." The friction that had resulted between English, Tory opinions and Reform-minded North American attitudes would be a rub throughout the century.

As I have remarked elsewhere, those were times when "intolerance was no crime and was in some instances elevated to a virtue." With its anti-French bias, powerful Orange Order, and a generally supportive attitude to the British Empire, Toronto was often seen as being bigoted and narrow-minded. One writer, by a strange twist of logic, ascribed success in business as being entirely due to "British pluck."

The backgrounds to such attitudes and opinions should always be kept in mind when reading history; all too often modern sensibilities are affronted by the blunt candour and biases of an earlier age. Historians, of course, are always only too happy to point out that to ignore the past may lead to its repetition.

With today's emphasis upon tolerance it is well to remember that the behaviour recorded in history reflects what Gibbon would have described as "the contagion of the times," and that Goethe had given a sardonic spin to the creed of tolerance with his perception that "to tolerate is to insult." It is interesting to reflect upon the "contagions" that might have created the biases and intolerance recorded in this book. There are usually reasons, tenuous though they may seem, for people's behaviour. That which benefits some does not necessarily benefit all.

The hopes for continued opportunities and the aspirations toward a "better world" were eroded by the Depression and collapsed in the spreading contagion of Nazism. In 1939 another era would come to an end, and I realized that for Yonge Street as for Toronto and Canada as a whole the succeeding new age would bring radical changes, both physical and in attitudes to the Street, the City, the Province and the Nation; it was the next terminal date, and what followed would be yet another story.

In conclusion, I should like to express my appreciation of the help given to me by the Archives of Ontario, the Toronto Metropolitan Library and the many Libraries and Historical Societies between Toronto and Penetanguishene. I also would like to thank the "200 Yonge" Committee, particularly Mrs. Mary Lloyd of the Richmond Hill Public Library, and Barry Penhale of Natural Heritage Books, who took the risky plunge of publishing this successor to *The Yonge Street Story*.

F. R. BERCHEM
Mississauga, Ontario
August, 1996

CHAPTER ONE

A COMMERCIAL STREET EMERGES

1860-1885

W hen Charles Dickens was a young, unknown reporter observing scenes of London life in the 1830s, one of his chief amusements was 'to watch the gradual progress—the rise and fall—of particular shops.' A sound instinct in a man with his gifts, because shops—great, small, dignified or dingy—have by their rise and fall marked the tides in human fashions and fortunes. From bazaars and tents by the caravan tracks, from solemn guild symbols in narrow, noisome, mediæval streets in the scents and spoils of Empire that scattered an aura of romance through London's gas-lit drabness, their story is a tale of hopes and ambitions, frustrations and failures.

The London of Dickens' setting was a grubby, vital, human one—the city of Bill Sikes, the soot, sin and squalor of 'the Rookery,' the dens and dives about St. Giles's and Covent Garden. With his quick eye for detail he saw a great deal of what many were quite happy to miss, and was a fair way on to becoming a star reporter.

What then happened to that ready eye during his visit to Toronto in 1842, when the, by that time, well-known novelist put up at the American Hotel on the northeast corner of Yonge and Front Streets? He said of Toronto that "the streets are well-paved and lighted with gas; the houses are large and good; the shops excellent." From what the inhabitants had to say of it, however, they obviously didn't share his enthusiasm, flattering though the description was.

The only street that had any sort of a reputation for shops was King. 'The

Corner' at its intersection with Yonge Street, where in 1820 had been the home and shop of Bostwick the wagon-maker, was the retail Mecca for fashionable Toronto. And surely Dickens, to reach there from his hotel, must have strolled past the stores and sights of lower Yonge Street. While 1842 was the year of the gas lamp on Toronto's streets, the stores along Yonge, what few there were and however well lit, could hardly be described as excellent.

Even by the 'sixties it couldn't be said that Yonge Street was very much to write home about, if at all, as far as shops were concerned. And the citizens loudly complained that they had "only one good piece of roadway in the whole city. ...the block pavement on King Street, between Yonge and Bay."[1] There were gripes about the ruts, stench and dirt of the city's streets in general—"Filth, filth is everywhere—A carter was seen throwing into a hollow place on Breadalbane, near Yonge, more than 5 large dead dogs and cats—where they lie uncovered giving off a horrid stench. The carter, in reply to objections said he had been instructed by the Corporation to throw them into any hole he might find in any of the streets."[2]

And added to that was the parade of perennial drunks, homeless, uninspired boozers and brawlers—"Martin Murray has been drunk from time immemorial, and was sent to gaol for seven days to get sobered up. John Haggard was mulcted in the sum of $5 for using the sidewalks for sleeping purposes, and Stampford Cull, who was labouring under delirium tremens, was remanded."[3] As the more common expression of those days went, Stampford had 'snakes in his boots.'

Those were the untouched facts of *The Globe*'s reports—if only there had been a young Dickens, like the Dickens who described the huddle of Irish labourers in one of London's seedier taverns, "who have been alternately shaking hands with, and threatening the life of each other for the last hour. ...and finding it impossible to silence one man, ...they resort to the expedient of knocking him down and jumping on him afterwards."

And like it or not, Toronto had its own local brew of such types, one of them, so the papers said, "A Dangerous Character,—James McLean, shoemaker of Yonge Street, gets drunk frequently, and under the influence invariably threatens or attempts to thrash his wife. Yesterday he got on one of his periodical drunks, and attempted to reorganize his 'better half,' who laid a complaint against him, and Policeman Osborne arrested him."[4]

In the 1860s the shoemakers were in the poky little boot and shoe stores that huddled on the east side of Yonge north of Adelaide. One of them had a brief notoriety during the Fenian troubles of 1866, "when a government detective arrested an employee, Thomas Sheedy. He was suspected of association with a colourful crew known as the Murphy men, a gang of Fenians then lodging in Cornwall gaol. At Sheedy's residence were found five revolvers, a sword and sword cane, and two hundred and ninety-nine dollars and fifteen cents."[5]

It was not Dickens the novelist, but Dickens the young reporter whom Toronto needed to describe its streets, stores and denizens, and no local writer with an equal descriptive ability existed. Instead, a picture must be put together from old newspapers, photographs and innumerable shallow reminiscences that shrink from the seamy vulgarity of the city. From all accounts Yonge Street in the 'sixties appears to have been a thin grey line of dingy and determined respectability separating some of the least salubrious stretches of lower Toronto.

As for the Yonge Street shops, they were far from excellent—all those dim, grubby, pinched little stores and taverns: confectioners, fruiterers, fishmongers and ale-bottlers; and below Adelaide Street was a proliferation of drug stores and dry goods outlets. It must have looked for all the world like Fagin's alley.

Running eastward was the notorious Stanley Street, one north of Adelaide and east of Yonge at Victoria. To the west, immediately adjoining Yonge at Queen Street and reaching to the University Avenue, was the nefarious St. John's Ward, described as being "at once the Negro quarter, the Five Points, and the St. Giles' of Toronto."[6] It included such unsavoury streets as Chestnut, Centre, Elizabeth and Dummer, forming an enclave of depravity in the eyes of sober and respectable citizens. Later, as with ships that have enjoyed a disastrous reputation, Dummer's name was changed—to William Street—and even changed a second time, I believe.

Dickens should have recognized it for what it was—a Little Dublin. It certainly wasn't Toronto the Good in those days, not by a very long shot. Trailing their coat-tails and religious differences through the many taverns of the town, the Irish made more noise than Finnegan's wake and their women drank, brawled and solicited their way to notoriety in the local press.

Two of them, Finnegan and O'Maly, (if you'll believe the names) were arrested for staging a bedlam of cursing, punching and pulling on Dummer Street. And contrary to a popular modern notion, the papers of the day had no hesitation in printing words that were then supposedly unprintable: "Sarah Morrison and Nelly Sloane, two prostitutes, were charged with being drunk and disorderly. The conduct of Sarah whilst in the dock was very disorderly."[7]

There was one sprig of a reporter, an anonymous employee of *The Daily Telegraph*, who did have a flair for making his subjects humorous, almost hilarious. He seems to have pursued his facts with a rare enthusiasm and related them with an equal gusto. He reported the court proceedings under the heading of 'The Justice Shop,' with one 'Beak McNabb' presiding and dispensing the justice.

One of the shop's customers, a Fanny Brunell, on being asked about her general status in society and what today might be called her lifestyle, produced the following testimonial to her character, according to the reporting wag:

> Manshin House
> Shtanley Shtreet, Joon 27, 1870
> This is to certify that I konsider Faney Brunnell is a dacent mimber
> av society and as ornimint to me conshtituency. She takes her's
> shtraight every time.
> J. D'oyle
> Mayer.[8]

It would be hard to get much closer than that to stage-Irish, but there's not much doubt about the types who made up the 'conshtituencies' bordering on downtown Yonge Street or their ways of life.

Another of the tribe of Lilith, an enterprising young woman, described in the classic style as a 'street cyprian,' beguiled a young man to a vacant lot on Church Street where he was relieved of his wallet and watch. At least she got away with her loot. A less lucky trio of Hibernian sylphs was scooped up before even coming within range of a likely victim—"Mary Ann Murphy, Emma Beaty and Mary Ann McDonald were arrested in the west end of the city on the watch for sailors, young men from the country, and other greenhorns to entrap and plunder. Murphy and McDonald were fined $4 or two months each, and Beaty $3 or two months. Her last words were—Spelt my name with one 't.'"[9]

Yonge Street was spared from forays by these hit-and-run commandos, but the occasional straggler livened things up, as when one evening "about five o'clock, a young woman of questionable reputation made an assault on a young man of considerable pretensions to gentility while he was promenading in the rain down Yonge street. A scene occurred; her umbrella was broken, his beaver fell a victim, her chignon was sacrificed, his face bled for its owner. An old gentleman separated the combatants; the female taking Queen street, her companion going straight home. Lacerated feelings and misplaced confidence caused the unpleasantness."[10]

Some of the reports were elaborated with all the Victorian trimmings about soiled lilies as the ladies of the night flitted through the prisoner's dock like bedraggled sparrows. The standard sentence was five dollars or thirty days, with which the courts tried to keep the streets of the city as tidy morally as physically, on the guiding principle that whatever wasn't visible, wasn't a problem. Public appearances were discouraged at every turn, even by punishment for association, "Allen Curry, a cabman, charged with driving women of bad character, was fined $2 and costs or ten days' imprisonment."[11]

The paradox in all of this, of course, was that if these women were so carefully kept out of sight, how were they recognized so easily? Not all of them were the blowzy, vermilion trollops of caricature; quite the reverse by the accounts of *The Daily Telegraph's* larky reporter, who showed a remarkably intimate knowledge of their 'unmentionable' way of life—A Madame Hinton kept a 'fashionable maison de plaisir' on Richmond Street near Yonge, and "Miss Jennie Vincent, one of our most talented and accomplished filles de joie whose elegantly furnished boudoir, with all the modern conveniences is pleasantly situated on University Street, was charged with using abusive language when in an elevated condition." On appearing before 'the Beak,' Jennie was described as looking "as luscious and insinuating as ever, but her beauty was slightly spoiled by a bruise on the left cheek, having had a row with her fancy man."[12] The 'Beak' was unmoved by her charms and delivered the usual 'five or thirty' option.

The more inelegant dens for diversion were disdained as mere bawdy houses and their customers were suspected of being threats to good order and public discipline, "Thomas Dunn, remanded on the charge of frequenting bawdy houses, was discharged."[13]

Toronto tried to keep its demimonde out of sight and thus out of mind, but the most ancient profession's age-old fascination for the prurient made it forever newsworthy. The racy reporting by *The Daily Telegraph's* man in the courts recognized this, but it would seem that the newspaper's publisher and proprietor, J. Ross Robertson, didn't approve of his employee's style. By the end of the fall of 1870 the reporter had either tidied up his act or had been fired, because his collection of misconduct then appeared under the heading of 'City Police' with Alex. McNabb, Esq., P.M. presiding in preference to 'The Beak.'

Maybe Robertson was right in easing up on the merriment, because these goings-on also had a dark and ugly side to them, as when the body of Annie Hill, a prostitute, was found with the head badly battered, in a field close to the Grand

Trunk Railway, near the Club House in Brockton village at what is now Dufferin Street.

And worse, perhaps, even if less sensational, was the tragic plight of the children, the forlorn waifs who peddled pathetic little bunches of flowers and papers on the streets in all weather, usually to provide the wherewithal for their parents' drinking sprees. Neglected, often beaten, they were the innocent victims of the viciousness engendered by hunger, filth and foul air. They were the very stuff of maudlin, Victorian melodrama—'Home, Sweet Home,' where 'there lies my fa—ather, drunk upon the floor.' If not passed out on the floor, he would probably beat his wife for complaining and kick the children for daring to be hungry.

The newsboys were the toughies among the street brats and some of them became almost legends, institutions of their day. Indulgently regarded as manly little fellows, they became the subjects of many local stories. Once a group of newsboys noticed a little girl shivering at an icy corner, with few customers for her bundle of papers. They clubbed together, bought her unsold stock, wrapped her up warmly and saw her safely home.

The great spot for newsboys was the corner at Yonge and King Streets. One of them, Davy O'Brien, had a stand there for years in the 'eighties and made a great success of it. Davy, so it was said, deposited "thirty dollars every two weeks in the Home Savings and Loan Company's office," and owned a house and lot on Duchess Street valued at eighteen hundred dollars. Such stories gained popularity as examples of how the poor could get ahead if they were willing to work and save.

For the unfortunate and the disabled, the only antidotes to their poverty were unpredictable charities and societies dedicated to the curtailment of drinking. In 1870 the Ontario Government had new sheds put up for the reception of newly arrived emigrants and that was about the limit of official concern. The business of health and welfare was then largely a matter of pot luck and local initiative by private citizens.

George Brown of *The Globe* used his paper in an active effort to expose some of the city's worst social injustices, particularly the abuse of children. Yet when reporting the death of a two-year old child on Bishop Street from starvation due to the extreme poverty of the parents, that paper could only offer the suggestion that "perhaps some benevolent citizen might be spurred to offer charitable assistance in such cases."[14]

When large numbers of emigrants arrived with scant funds and few skills, however, the demands of poverty strained even the sympathies of the charitable.

Even *The Globe* during January, 1877 complained about the "continual racket" that was being made over the troubles of the poor. As any observer of human society well knows, whenever the requests for the relief of poverty seem to become insatiable, there is a backlash of frustrated and uncooperative reaction from those who once were sympathetic. Henri-Frédéric Amiel described it best when he said that "moral indifference is the malady of the cultivated classes."

Yet many of the individual tales were pathetic and moving in their evidence of human dignity struggling to stand against all odds. A family of three was discovered one night outside the police station at 319 Yonge Street opposite Agnes (Dundas Street West). The mother and small daughter had settled themselves in a wheelbarrow and the father had seated himself on the ground beside it, all of them ill-clad for the temperatures of the coming night. When questioned by the police, the father said that they were on their way from Hamilton to Collingwood, where he had hopes of finding work. They had no more possessions than what they had with them and only a few dollars in cash. The father had a letter from the mayor of Hamilton, on the basis of which he hoped that Toronto's mayor might give him some assistance to reach Collingwood. It was a sorry little epistle of hope, with nothing of the brash humour of Fanny Brunell's 'certificate of character.'

The facts seldom needed much embellishment. Oscar Wilde once cracked that a person would need to have a heart of stone not to be overcome by helpless laughter when reading the death scene of Dickens' Little Nell. That was Dickens the novelist overdoing it with his descriptions. Dickens the reporter would have found the stark facts sufficient to create effect. One wonders how much he really saw of Toronto, where life for the poor was an incessant struggle of despair, and very much a matter of devil take the hindmost, with a temporary oblivion provided by drinking and brawling.

The ethics of the dour Scots and sharp-nosed Yankee merchants of Yonge Street held that a man was what he made of himself and they weren't slow to use themselves as examples of bootstrap-hoisting to prosperity in Toronto, the city of opportunity. Ability and hard work will be rewarded, was their creed, inspired by such pawky Scots' proverbs as, 'mony a meikle mak's a muckle'—a treasury of shrewdness in a language that defied the best efforts of others to understand it.

And it wasn't by any means a new creed. Scots merchants had been chasing the favours of business almost since the time of Toronto's founding, with William

Allan as perhaps the best and most successful of their ambitious breed. While Allan had had several schemes and ploys always on the bubble, however, the new influx of the 'fifties and 'sixties stuck to one line of business, in many cases, that of dry goods.

They were not to be confused with the likes of those tattery-breek'd Highland laddies who had screwed a fortune out of the fur trade that combined romance and adventure with account-ledger tallies. This was strictly wholesale and retail business, with no frills and no sentiment, only the clang of the cash register. And they were more numerous than in the past, these Scots, especially in Toronto where storekeepers rivalled and jockeyed one another in the scramble to success, with many a cry-halloo as opportunity started fortune's hares.

Storekeeping was a chancy game, as the crises of 1847 and 1857 had shown. Yonge Street became, if you like, Toronto's early version of what is now commonly called the rat-race. The city's fledgling stage had ended. By the late 'sixties Toronto was spreading its wings as a trading capital. With Confederation in 1867 it also became the official capital of the new Province of Ontario, the former Upper Canada. Its citizens brashly touted its merits while outsiders gave thumbs down to its pretensions. If the aristocratic stretch of King Street was how Torontonians like to imagine their achievements, others saw them more in terms of pushy, middle-class Yonge Street.

Freeland's Soap & Candle Factory - Foot of Yonge St. (1832-65)

At the bottom of Yonge Street, but by no means at the bottom of the commercial heap, overlooking the Bay, was the Freeland soap and candle factory. Peter Freeland was a long-lipped, canny Scot from Glasgow, that Western Ocean trading terminus where tight-mouthed merchants shrewdly hedged the hazards of the shipping game, about the closest that these good Presbyterians ever came to poker.

Peter made a tidy profit out of the soap-boiling and candle-making business between 1832 and 1865, combining it with the pleasure of shooting ducks in the Bay from the doorways of his premises. It must have been a pleasant enough spot at first, down there by the water, away from the clutter and smells of the growing town, with at least a hint of romance in the sight of ships beating up for the harbour. A Glasgow man, remembering the traffic of his own River Clyde, would appreciate that—but it was not to be that way for long.

The age of sail, soft-soap and candles was on the wane as new advances were made in transport and industry. By the time that the Great Western Railway's extension from Hamilton had been put through to Toronto with a terminus at the foot of Yonge Street there were new prospects for development. Peter Freeland's factory closed in 1865. His name, however, lives on in Freeland Street on the east side of the present 'Star' building at number one Yonge Street.

Railways, steamships and telegraphs were all very splendid and progressive in the opinion of the good citizens of Toronto, but progress soon made their waterfront one of the less attractive areas of the Bay. Just as the salmon in his native Clyde had been done for by industry's leavings, so the ducks were put paid to by something a lot more lethal than Peter Freeland's old fowling-piece.:

> The solid matter which has been conveyed down the Yonge street sewer into the bay has accumulated between Milloy's and the adjoining wharf to the depth of six feet, and consequently the filthy stuff must be dredged out again. As this work has to be done annually some idea may be had of the state of the bay.[15]

The Milloys had succeeded the Freelands as kings of the heap at the foot of Yonge Street. They were wharfingers, shipping and steamboat agents with their wharf at the Esplanade between Scott and Yonge Streets. To reach the wharf from the Esplanade meant crossing the spread of railway tracks that had ruined any hopes of making the Esplanade into a waterfront attraction for visitors and pleasure-strollers.

THE STEAMER
CITY OF TORONTO
CAPTAIN D. MILLOY

The Steamer
City of Toronto
Captain D. Milloy

Will leave Yonge Street Wharf every morning (Sunday's excepted)
at 7 o'clock for Niagara and Lewiston, connecting with Express
trains on the Erie and Niagara, and New York Central Railroads
for Suspension Bridge Falls, Buffalo, New York, Boston, & c.—
Also at Buffalo with Lake Shore Railroad and Steamers.
    Tickets and further information at No. 8 Front Street, Toronto.

N. Milloy
Agent.[16]

It was the 'City of Toronto,' her ensign at half-mast, that docked at the
crowded Yonge Street wharf in the hot stillness of the night of June 3, 1866 with
the dead and wounded from the engagement with the Fenians at Ridgeway.

Great Western Railway Station ~ foot of Yonge Street.
built 1866 ~ taken over by CN and used as a freight depot
until 1896 ~ then a fruit depot until burned in 1952.
Now the site of the O'Keefe Centre.

Nichol Milloy, who boarded at the nearby American Hotel on Yonge Street, was the agent for the Canadian Inland Navigation Company. By the 'eighties Donald—with names like that they had to be from Peter Freeland's country where Milloy was a frequent name in Lowland Scotland—was the representative for the Richelieu and Ontario Navigation Company. The latter absorbed the Inland Navigation Company and became the largest inland steamship company in Canada, with a fleet of some twenty-five ships, six of them plying between the Yonge

Geddes' (No. 1) Wharf – Yonge Street. – c. 1900.

Street wharf and Montreal, and the balance trading on the St. Lawrence River.

With the thump and thrash of paddle-wheel and propeller in the harbour and the snort of locomotives shunting near the wharves, the waterfront at Yonge Street broadcast the city's entry into the sweepstakes of progress, the natural harbour giving Toronto a long lead over the other locations along Lake Ontario's shore from Kingston to Hamilton. This indeed was progress.

Tennyson prattled on about progress proceeding merrily down "the ringing grooves of change," his poetic metaphor for the monotonous clack and clatter of railways that heralded breakthroughs for man's welfare. The changes, however, would not always be a reformer's dream come true, as Tennyson himself realized when not befuddled by his diet of old port and shag tobacco.

There was certainly a considerable difference in Yonge Street's situation and fortunes, to the benefit of business and to the disadvantage of taste. It could no longer survive solely on the hopes of becoming a great highway for trade to the north. The best freight route to Lake Huron and Georgian Bay was provided by the Northern Railroad, the Toronto progressives' darling that shared a station with the Grand Trunk and Great Western Railways at the bottom of York Street until 1871.

And as an axis for population spreading north, the Yonge Street road had withered in contrast with the early expectations for it. The spread went east-west along the lakefront and from the city's core. With the growth of commerce at the southern end of the street there also came a sharper contrast between the business interests in the city and the farmers whose lands rolled out into the country from only five miles north of Queen Street. It emphasized the split that had been evident between government authority and the Yonge Street farmers in the 1837 Rebellion.

Yonge Street really arrived commercially in the boom of the 'sixties, sweeping from the fashionless 'fifties toward the elegant 'eighties. What had been planned in its beginnings as a military highway northward to complement an east-west military road—then Dundas, later Queen Street—had become a purely commercial thoroughfare at its city end by the 'sixties.

If Johnny Simcoe could have seen the 'sixties, he'd have had the stutters over his blessed Yonge Street—its lower end, at any rate. He had never had much enthusiasm for tradesmen at the best of times, but pushy Scots merchants had been one of his pet peeves, notably a Robert Hamilton of Niagara. Now they were not only becoming successful, but respectable too, dammit—the Colonel wouldn't have like that, sir.

And in truth, some of the encomium is a bit hard to take in retrospect. With thudding Victorian rhetoric, a Pelham Mulvany had this to say of Toronto in the late nineteenth century:

> The interesting features of Toronto. ...are due chiefly to the liberality
> and culture of the business men, from whom is obtained the money
> required to carry to completion all material improvement. It is true
> that many professional men give money to aid great works, but it
> will be found, if traced back sufficiently, that this money was earned
> by them directly or indirectly from business men.[17]

This rather smarmy tone left its treacly trail on the pages of many contemporary histories of the city, as in this comment by Mercer Adam;

> If there is ever a breath of repining, it may come from a man of
> education and brains, who has been misguided enough to take to
> intellectual pursuits for a living, instead of going into the liquor
> traffic, keeping an hotel or becoming a sugar-broker's clerk.[18]

The almost rabid obsession with democracy would have amazed Simcoe more than it might have shocked him. To quote Mulvany once more:

> Though so essentially and vitally democratic, this is truly an age of kings. We hear constantly of money kings, railway kings, cotton kings and many other varieties of monarch, the claim to the royal title being not any blue-blood heredity, but in general, simply that triumph of well-directed personal industry which is within the reach of every man on this free American continent, however humble or obscure, who proves himself able and worthy to achieve it. This glorious Dominion can boast of few such kings, and among them there is one gentleman who has fairly earned the title to rank as the Canadian dry goods king. This gentleman is Mr. John Macdonald, the founder of the great dry goods house of John Macdonald & Co., of Toronto and Manchester. He owes it to his own high business qualities—among which regard may be had to his sterling character as well as to his shrewdness and enterprise— that, through a long vista of commercial failures, he can look back upon a career of unbroken success. ...
>
> ...Mr. Macdonald's success is just an example of the possibilities that are open to any young man in Canada whose chief capital consists of brains, self-reliance, energy, and above all, integrity.[19]

Mulvany also couldn't resist a dig at "the injustice of Upper Canada College being maintained at the expense of the 'raw democracy' as a hot-house for fastening on our school system an alien and noxious growth of shoddy aristocracy. ..."[20]

There is a suspicion that some of the notions of democracy resulted from chewing the seeds of sour grapes. However, no opportunity to wallow in eulogies upon democracy was to be missed, even although the writer might be rather shaky on the implications of the theory of democracy. It was, after all, the Greeks who had given substance to the idea, described by Thucydides as being a way to check the powerful and to provide a refuge for the weak,—but American sages transformed it into a glorification of the work ethic, or how to succeed without feeling guilty.

Shopkeeping was to provide the pattern for what might be called Toronto's aristocracy, a far cry from the hereditary breed that Simcoe had wanted to establish in his Province of Upper Canada. Old Carnegie himself couldn't have better expressed than Mulvany the rags to riches figment of the American Dream. Hard work was Toronto's progenitor and opportunity was its middle name. Heaven help any native sons who were guilty of backsliding on their jobs! "William Newell and James Still, charged with leaving the employment of Messrs. E. & C. Gurney without permission, were fined $2 each without costs."[21]

The 'old guard,' the descendants of Simcoe's retinue, the Robinsons, Jarvises, Ridouts and Smalls, and later the Baldwins and Denisons, still considered themselves to be *the* élite of Toronto. They were, however, willing to accept and absorb new recruits from business, such as the Mulocks, Howlands and Gooderhams. Although they admired British ways, they were not so far gone as to be like Mrs. Bute Crawley in Thackeray's *Vanity Fair*, who vowed that she would "never give the pas to a tradesman's daughter."

Indeed, 'old' families had gone happily into business themselves. D'Arcy Boulton kept a shop in Toronto. Peter Robinson had owned a store in Newmarket. The Ridout nephews had a hardware store since the 1830s on the northeast corner of Yonge and King Streets, an excellent choice of spot for the business that in 1867 became Ridout, Aikenhead and Crombie until 1876, when Ridout sold out to the other two.

Among the more notable of these early successes was that of a Yorkshireman, Joseph Bloor, who in the 'twenties had been the landlord of the Farmer's Arms near Toronto marketplace. Upon retiring from there, he started a brewery in the ravine north of the second concession road near Yonge where Severn Street now runs. From that he profited handsomely and formed a partnership in land speculation with Sheriff Jarvis, the result of their efforts being the village of Yorkville. The village came within a whisker of being called Bloorville, but in the end only the second concession road was named Bloor Street after the brewer.

Naming streets after brewers! How Simcoe would have shuddered at that one, but it was the forerunner of the pattern to come. At the beginning of Toronto's development, in 1796, the area around Yonge and Bloor Streets had been known as Playterville after the first settler there, the old Loyalist Quaker, Captain George Playter. He had Lot 20 that was bounded by what later became Yonge Street on the west, the old Don Mills Road on the east and Bloor Street on the south. Captain Playter's house was located immediately north of Castle Frank. Fifty years later and the old Loyalists were making way for a new breed of which Bloor was an early example.

Bloor's daughter, Elizabeth, made a propitious marriage to a soundly established Toronto lawyer, Joseph Curran Morrison, later Judge Morrison. Morrison bought

Ridout's - #73 Yonge Street - King Corner, 1876.

the property known as Woodlawn that stood on the west side of Yonge at what is now Woodlawn Avenue from his law partner, William Blake. On a passing note, this was the William Hume Blake who acted as Crown Prosecutor in the November, 1843 trials of James McDermot and Grace Marks for the murder of their master, Thomas Kinnear, and his housekeeper, at their home on Yonge Street near Richmond Hill.

To return to the theme, Toronto's society was most certainly a mobile one for those who could take advantage of its opportunities and by the 1860s these had increased with the growing demands upon business. Enthusiastic writers about Toronto would ascribe success in business "entirely to British pluck."[22] A somehow divinely-dispensed commodity that put a seal of approval upon the profits from hard work and enterprise.

Unfortunately for the enthusiasts, it was not conveniently so arranged. Business in Toronto during the first half of the 'sixties was helped in a fair way by American agents making purchases of stores for the armies in the Civil War. And while well-to-do Americans avoided service by paying out three hundred dollars in bribes, scores of less affluent 'skedaddlers' dodged over the border into Canada.

These 'skedaddlers' found work wherever they could. Some of them worked on building Oaklands, the home of Mulvany's merchant hero, Mr. John Macdonald, now the site of De La Salle school on Avenue Road south of St. Clair Avenue. At that date, 1860, Avenue Road was more of a hazard than a road and the east-west

Davenport south of Oaklands was little beyond a memorial to an old Indian trail. Consequently a long driveway had to run from the Macdonald home to Yonge Street.

John Macdonald was top rooster of the run of those long-headed Scots mer chants who had started out in Canada about the middle of the nineteenth century, prospered, and built splendid homes and were styled 'merchant princes.' And for many of them, Yonge Street was their wash-pot.

Macdonald was born in Perth, Scotland in 1824. He came to Toronto Barracks as a boy with his father who, as a hospital sergeant in the 93rd, the Sutherland Highlanders, was garrisoned there from 1838 to 1843. Son John stayed behind when the troops went back to Scotland. He worked as a salesman for Walter Macfarlane's Victoria House on King Street, at the same time studying for the Wesleyan Methodist ministry to which he had become a convert from his native Presbyterian Church.

There is a story that the father returned to Toronto where he set up a druggist's store on Yonge Street near Shuter in 1846. That was about the time when the son was found to be suffering from consumption and for the good of his health went to the West Indies, where he stayed for about two years. The standard of morals there disgusted him.

On coming back to Toronto in 1849, John Macdonald started the first retail dry goods store on Yonge Street at number 103 (old numbering) near Richmond Street. Always a dabbler in poetry, he advertised his new venture in verse:

> Will you call at Macdonald's, if only to try,
> From his well-sorted stock, how cheap you can buy?

The business prospered and around 1853 he was able to sell out to a Marmaduke Pearson before moving to a larger building at 30 Wellington Street East where he dealt in wholesale dry goods. He made a sizable fortune in his busi ness, but remained plain and economical in his private life.

His photographs show a long-sided parallelogram of a Scots face with a Kirk- disciplined nose. There was a frigid passion about his beliefs that would have given the shivers to Old Nick himself; an avoidance of "theatres, operas, saloons, cigars, cabs, horse hire and expensive trappings in clothes."[23] How dreary! He would have been horrified by the Miss McCormick who bought Oaklands from the Macdonald family and, so the story goes, indulged in the extravagance of keeping an entire Negro orchestra of her own on the premises.

From a gloomy little Yonge Street haberdashery at the 'Large 103,' John Macdonald had waxed into financial splendour. He was active in the Board of Trade and became a director of the Canadian Bank of Commerce whose first president was William McMaster, an Irishman who also had made good early in the great dry goods bonanza that started on Yonge Street.

With Macdonald's business success went a great interest in good works and deserving causes. An abstainer himself, he was much in sympathy with the Temperance movement, supporting the City Christian Temperance Mission and the more militant Prohibitory Alliance. The Salvation Army he at first thought to be a bit too much Hallelujah, bang the drum, Sister Hannah, but after he became aware of the good work that was accomplished by them, he gave it his favour.

John Macdonald, in fact, personified the strong bond that developed between business and religion in Toronto during the 1860s. When he moved to Oaklands, he associated with the Bloor Street Methodist Church and was instrumental in securing the ground for a church which was built on Yonge Street at Marlborough Avenue.

By 1875, when 'Jno. Macdonald, a commercial man,' is being boosted by his contemporaries to go for a place in the Dominion Parliament, he has without a doubt, 'arrived,' although he treated politics more as a stern duty than as an hon-

John Macdonald's
103 Yonge Street
(1849–1853)

" 'Tis a three-storey house, with
    the front painted white,
Which makes its appearance
         both graceful and light
With very large figures that
    you plainly may see,
Describing his number as
    one hundred and three."

our. In a letter to his wife in 1878 he described, with obvious disapproval, the antics of the House of Commons in Ottawa where he was sitting as a Member:

> Members banged desk-lids, playing the 'devil's tattoo;' made creaking noises, sang songs, blew whistles, shouted and roared. All order was lost, and confusion rampant. The night wore on, Here and there were groups of men using high words, and excited with drink.[24]

Progress had yet to catch up with civilization.

In 1887 he reached his pinnacle as Senator, the Honourable John Macdonald, the only Liberal to be appointed to the Senate by his friend and namesake, Sir. John A. Macdonald. It was a considerable achievement and a long way indeed from the salesboy in Macfarlane's, but Macdonald never lost his pride in his humble origins.

Always interested in the encouragement of the young, he gave the YMCA the full benefit of his philosophy and business wisdom. In the archives of Ontario there is a copy of one of his talks, given probably in the old Shaftesbury Hall on

Yonge Street Methodist Church.   from Robertson's 'Landmarks'.

Queen Street West. The title was *Business Success* and the dry goods czar told his audience that, "it should be acknowledged that the son of a coal-heaver has as much right to aim at the best positions in the land, as the son of a lord." Hardly a novel theory in Canada or elsewhere at that time, but Mulvany would have loved to hear it. If anything, however unintentional, there was a Darwinian flavour in the implication that the unsuccessful perish.

The young men of the YMCA were also told to marry early and 'marry in your own station.' And that was pretty much the same sort of advice that Tennyson's Northern Farmer passed on to his son: "Doänt thou marry for munny, but goä wheer munny is." The money was there on Yonge Street, even if there wasn't any style.

Money—there is a Senecan sourness in that old Latin tag, "Qui festinat ad divitias, non erit insons," with its implied damnation of all businessmen as scoundrels that would have delighted Karl Marx. Horace, too, had called 'Queen Money' the taint of Ancient Rome, but in the self-styled Queen City of Toronto, money was the ultimate blessing.

This pursuit of money was not an unalloyed endeavour, its flaws being pointedly expressed by one contemporary writer:

> Everything gives way to business. Private neighbourhoods are constantly being encroached upon for the purpose of business; which is steadily advancing towards the extremities of the city, north, east and west. ...while the visiting merchant sees only the smooth and finished side of the picture, it is none the less true that there is a dark side to it also. He should see the struggles of the employees in the houses he visits to keep themselves in clothing, and the necessaries of life, and to submit to the overbearing manner and petty tyranny of some one who has had the good fortune to get into a position of trust.[25]

They may have been an honest enough lot, these early Yonge Street merchants, given the several tributes to their integrity. Yet the honesty may have been a part of a somewhat uncompromising, rigid ethic with little tolerance for backsliding and the flesh's frailties. Their eye was ever steady on the main chance, the bargain to be grasped. And there must always be the suspicion that Seneca may have been right after all. The Scots particularly have a tendency to look with dour disapproval upon the evidences of great wealth.

When that sturdy old Aberdonian, Bishop Strachan, proudly showed his brother James the splendid home, 'the Palace,' that he had built in 1818 at York and Front Streets, the cautious James' comment was, "I hope it's a' come by honestly, John." Like the ruined works of Ozymandias, 'the Palace' in time deteriorated to a shell of its original grandeur, becoming at the last a boarding house before being destroyed in 1900.

Another Scot who climbed to a lofty perch on the commercial ladder was a 'townie' of Bishop Strachan—John Catto, who, when he died at the age of ninety-five in 1928, was described as 'the dean of Toronto merchants.' He was born in Fraserburgh, Aberdeen, Scotland's 'Granite City' where they say that even the seagulls won't follow an Aberdeen trawler because nothing is ever thrown overboard.

And from the looks of his photographs, old John Catto wouldn't have thrown much, if anything, overboard either. Although from farm stock, he came from an area famous for its rugged, hard-driving, 'Pe'erheid' whalers and fishermen, in a land where nature carved people the way she carved the rocks. There was a hard-eyed, flinty-featured set to these men, like a chip from one of the buildings in their native city. They didn't take contradiction kindly.

John Catto made his way at nineteen to St. John's, Newfoundland in 1852. There he worked as a salesman for Brocking, Son and Company for two years before following the Scotsman's rainbow road to Upper Canada. Reaching Toronto in 1854 he shrewdly apprenticed to one of the city's leading linen drapers and dry goods merchants, Peter Patterson.

With an almost relentless energy and drive that was to be found in a fair number of his countrymen in Canada, he learned his business thoroughly. If the English produced young administrators, the Scots came early to business leadership in Toronto. John Macdonald had opened his first store on Yonge Street when he was twenty-five. John Catto, with 'Quality before Quantity' as his battle-cry, started his own dry goods wholesale and retail store at 116 Yonge Street near the corner of Adelaide in 1862, when he was twenty-nine.

The older heads that had nodded in doubt at such youthful enterprise had to admit his ability, however, when after two years John Catto has done well enough to be able to shift to the much more fashionable King Street, at number 59 east.

Here he advertised 'Cashmere and Lamb's Wool Hosiery, Eider Down Comfortables, Skirts and Coseys,'—'Nottingham lace curtains, and new white bed quilts.' Himself immaculate in frock coat, he was in his shop each day, almost to the time of his death, overseeing his charge like a good shipmaster, ready for any challenge. Outliving all his contemporaries, he was a long established figure of the commercial scene and the retailer 'par excellence' of linen.

He developed a unique line by importing clan and family tartans from Scotland whose nostalgic natives cling to Auld Lang Syne like porridge to a ladle. For his part he was very fond of the national anthem, "Scots Wha Ha'e," detested the bagpipes and noted with a businessman's eye and an ironic relish the American enthusiasm for all manner of Scots trappings: kilts, sporrans, bonnets and buckles.

Unlike those of Yankee stock, whose sole loyalties were usually to money and land, these two Highland Scots, Macdonald and Catto, had in them that fierce national pride in the valour of the Scottish soldier, unglamorously described by some as the world's last savage. Macdonald thrilled to the feats of the old 93rd, the "thin red line" at Balaclava and the saviours of Lucknow. He did a great deal to encourage the establishment of the 48th Highlanders of Toronto, created after his death and affiliated with the Gordon Highlanders of the British Army. A large painting of the Gordon Highlanders in action at Dargai on the North West Frontier of India still hangs in the mess of the Toronto regiment. John Catto's only son was a major in the 48th. Bishop Strachan, however, didn't share their national affection for the military. It was only with great reluctance that he bought his son, James McGill Strachan, a commission in the British Army for £1,500.

Like Macdonald, John Catto was not an extravagant man, but was perhaps even more single-minded in his devotion to his business, and equally sympathetic to worthwhile charities. Although a devout man, he was less openly fervent in his attitude than Macdonald and described himself simply as a 'Churchman,' a member of the Scottish Episcopalian Church. As a 'Piscy' he was a great admirer and friend of Bishop Strachan and often told the story that it was he who was responsible for deciding the name for the girls' school in memory of the late Bishop. At least, that was his way of it. He was for a long time a member of Holy Trinity Church on Yonge Street.[26]

In 1922 John Catto sold his King Street property to the King Edward Hotel Company and moved back to Yonge Street, number 219-223 at the corner of Shuter, not far from the site of his first independent venture. When he died, the T. Eaton Company put a black-bordered tribute in the Toronto newspapers on a full page that was empty of any other notice. He had never set foot inside Eaton's or Simpson's himself, believing that their wares were really rather 'junky.' However that may be, he was worthy of his tribute, the last of a dry goods breed that had included such stars as John Macdonald, Gordon, Mackay, Simpson and Eaton—even Eaton's early forebears had been Scots.

The tide in the affairs of Yonge Street ran strongly in favour of the dry goods merchants on the lower part of the street at the start of the 'sixties. And true to Brutus's remark to Cassius, when taken at the flood it led to fortune for a fair number of them. The Cattos and Macdonalds got their start on the street and then moved on.

Shortly after 1866, more of the dry goods people began to cast around for better premises and locations, some removing entirely from Yonge Street to more modish milieus. Others pooled their talents and resources, the better to meet the growing competition.

To stand and be still was about as fatal as the famous Birkenhead Drill when it came to commercial competition on Yonge Street as storekeepers jostled for the

Old Grantham Store –170 Yonge Street – c.1874.   from Robertson's 'Landmarks'.

most favourable stands on its city length. For a time, shops and businesses changed hands and sites as fast as a tinker's blessing.

Take, for example, number 170 Yonge Street, on the west side between Queen and Richmond, that had been Grogan's boot and shoe store sometime in the 'fifties. In 1861 it became Ed Grantham's saloon which he changed to a lamp and rock-oil store in 1864. Then by 1870 he was retailing Winsor and Newton's tube colours. By early 1872 Grantham had established himself well enough that he could remove to number 78 King Street West, where he sold artists' materials and lamp goods. Thereafter the shop on Yonge Street became a shooting gallery, stationer's and tobacconist's until its demise around 1890. Dickens would have enjoyed watching that, as he would the generally hectic, shifting scene on the Yonge Street of the 'sixties.

It was a busy spot, to be sure, but the blight upon this hive of industry was worse than any swarm upon Pharaoh's crops—drink was the rot of business's fibre.

Some joker of those days said that the curse of Canada was drink. And for sources of supply, Yonge Street in the 'sixties was not at any great remove from its pioneer days of hostelries, inns, malt and suds. The Street started respectably enough at its lower end with the American Hotel, famous for its cuisine and patronized by such as Dickens and prominent members of the theatrical world. Although one Toronto citizen who disapproved of novelists as being the smallest of the literary fry was delighted when the author of *Sketches by Boz* departed from Toronto without much public fuss having been made over him. Like the stores that Dickens enjoyed watching, the American Hotel changed hands as frequently as a juggler's cup and saucer act.

When Dickens and his wife stayed there in 1842 the hotel was almost brand-new like the Cunarder *'Britannia'* in which they had crossed the Atlantic. By 1861 the American was being run by Patterson and Walker, then early in the 'seventies Walker left to start the equally well-known Walker House at Front and University that was torn down in 1976. A George Brown was running the American in 1875, with rooms going for two dollars a day, then it was again advertised to let, with possession on May 1, 1880.

In 1883 it was rather appropriately turned over to an American, James H,. Mackie, 'formerly of New York and New Orleans,' by his father William who was then the proprietor. The younger Mackie also managed the Hotel Hanlan on Toronto Island, owned by Ned Hanlan the champion oarsman who in 1884 was

The American Hotel ~ Yonge & Front ~ 1880.

on a visit to Australia, where he was defeated on the Paramata River course. In its setting close to the wharves, the American must have been a popular spot with the United States tourists who came up from Niagara in droves during the summer season. However, it lasted but a bare half century, being demolished in 1889.

Going north on the east side of Yonge Street were the less exotic, but more locally popular hotels-cum-inns such as the Bay Horse at number 137-9, run by Thomas Best in 1861 and long a favourite stopping-off place for farmers coming in from Hogg's Hollow. C. Brelsford was the proprietor in 1876, and shortly thereafter, about 1883 it was knocked down along with some adjacent buildings to make way for the more prestigious Yonge Street Arcade, but the name lived on, apparently being transferred to the old Globe Hotel.

The Globe, at number 163 between Richmond and Queen Streets, was another favourite resort for a quiet and casual noggin, especially after the more notorious Rob Roy Hotel became defunct in the 'fifties. The Globe had a string of proprietors: R. Varcoe in 1861, Mrs. Gardiner, Samuel Thompson and, in 1876, N. Robinson.

When the Bay Horse was demolished to make way for the Arcade, it would seem that T.J. Best, the son of the Bay Horse's old proprietor Thomas, then took over the Globe Hotel and changed its name to the Bay Horse. This reincarnated Bay Horse was badly damaged in the great fire of March, 1895 and was finally broken up in 1909.[27]

Of lesser standing, but closer to the old days of pot-hoisting and roistering, was the Green Bush Inn, probably started in the pioneering era by the well-known but never apparently too successful Joseph Abraham whose original inn of that name was on the northeast corner of what is now Yonge and Steeles Avenue. The downtown Green Bush was at number 215-17 near the southeast corner of Shuter Street, and in 1876 its proprietor was J. Conley. Sometime about 1880, when it was managed by John Hirst, the name was changed to the Russell House and it enjoyed a brief spell of prominence.

It also had a flirt with notoriety in the newspapers when one of its employees was shot in the arm. John Woods, an ostler at the Russell House, was carousing with his buddies one night in February, 1883 at Mrs. Tullidale's saloon on Albert Street. There he and another character called Rice had a falling-out, and the argument continued when they carried on to Schole's nearby on Yonge Street. Back again to Mrs. Tullidale's and Rice pulled a revolver from his pocket and shot Woods. The wound was patched up, Woods went back to work, and no arrests were made.[28]

Russell House, for no real reason, seems to be an unfortunate choice of name for hostels, because these so often tend to become run-down and seedy—tatty reminders of an elusive respectability.

As for the rest of the east side of Yonge Street in the city, it was belly to the bar, boys, bang for your beer and bolt it back,—at number 153, the Carlton Saloon, at Goldsmith's Dew Drop Inn number 223, now the site of the Silver Rail on the north side of Shuter, or at the tritely named Yonge Street Inn at 261 opposite Alice Street.

Near the northern city limits of Bloor Street, more precisely the second building below Charles Street (East), was the most decrepit of all, the Gardener's Arms,—so dilapidated, in fact, that it wasn't mentioned in the 1876 Street Directory. It stood in an area that, north of Wood Street, was a clutter of saddlers, tinsmiths, lumber merchants, private homes and variety stores. At 483-85 were the Pims: Hy, John and Jno., iron workers and wagon makers.

The Gardener's Arms never enjoyed any great renown, at one time being kept by 'a Mr. Abraham,' probably he of the Green Bush Inn. In the 'sixties it was run by one Parker, 'a genuine, crusty Englishman,' whatever that may mean—hardly a reference for mine host of the florid bonhomie. Joseph Jackes had the place in 1873, following which it gradually degenerated to premises for an old wagon shop and yard. Like the creaking gate that hangs longest, however, the collapse of the shell that was the Gardener's Arms did not come until 1924, outlasting many a better-found place.[29]

Crossing over to the west side of Yonge Street and a short distance south of Bloor was the old Rising Sun Hotel at number 666, another survivor from the pioneer days, managed by a Jackson in the 'sixties, and J. Burgess in 1876. And continuing south, while the water supply could have been as scarce as that for the Ancient Mariner, there were enough liquor outlets for a fleet's crew—eight more hotels and three saloon-taverns, straggling down to Louisa Street. Little wonder that, if they chose, fair numbers of the working population in the city could get as drunk as Paddy's pig.

Names changed, proprietors came and went like the weather. At number 448 Yonge Street was the Avenue Hotel, proprietor George Gray who had the Victoria, possibly the same hotel, in that area in the 'sixties. On the corner of Hayter Street, where Hussey had the Schomberg Inn about the year 'sixty-one, was Townley's Saloon in 1876.

Mackinson's Hotel, near the southwest corner of Yonge and Elm Streets, became the White Hart Hotel, proprietor Bell Belmont and manageress Emma Belmont. In the next block, on the corner of Edward Street, James MacFarland had the Royal Arms that had been Henwood's old hotel in the 'sixties. Where King Street had high-class grocers such as Fulton, Michie and Company retailing fine wines and sherries in an abundance that would have delighted Gilbert and Sullivan's Gondoliers, Yonge Street had a boozers' corridor.

Before the Street began a stagger toward a greater respectability during the 'sixties, a character called old Tom Rutledge sold bottled ale and porter at number 89 Yonge Street. The McCormack Brothers has their Ontario Ale and Porter Vaults on the corner of Elm Street where thirsty customers bought their brews in pints and quarts. By 1876 the McCormacks were more respectably set up as grocers at number 431 Yonge Street.

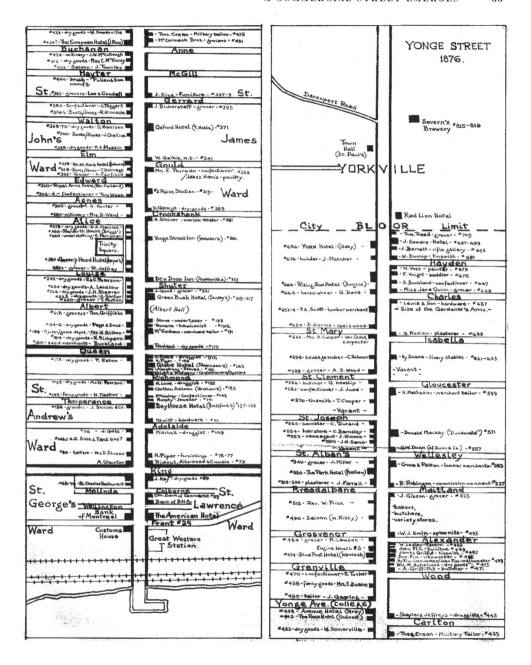

The reaction to all of this was inevitable; a massive temperance movement. Movement?—it became a virtual crusade. Drinking in Toronto may have been a dour, dismal practice with an almost Calvinist determination to make it as joyless as possible, like putting salt on porridge. But the Temperance reaction was equally grim and holy, pitching its tents near Yonge Street's battle-line of boozers.

In the early pioneering days, drink itself had been a salvation from drudgery and discomfort, and so sat lightly on the public conscience. Then, it had been a rare individual who stood out against alcohol. The most notable example was Jessie Ketchum, the tanner, who in 1832 had given the ground on which the Upper Canada Religious Tract Society set up its headquarters on Yonge Street, where it was still going strong in the 'seventies at number 102.

By the 'sixties drink had become increasingly associated with poverty, degradation and that bogey of industry, sloth, so that more and more of Toronto's solid citizens supported religious temperance meetings. These didn't provide any solution to the problems that encouraged drinking, they merely denounced alcohol and tried to prohibit it by decree. Democracy was a grand thing, my friend, but no respectable citizen of Toronto would accept the definition of it that allowed the right of everyone 'to go to hell in his own way.'

In the 'sixties Toronto experienced the beginning of the stirrings of what has always alarmed the free-spirited, an enthusiasm for creating goodness by legislation. This really hit its stride with the Scott Act and the Cooks Act in the early 'eighties.

There may have been howls of delight when John A. Macdonald told a political gathering that he was a better man drunk than George Brown sober—a statement that

From an old drawing of Fire Hall No. 3 at 476 Yonge Street — (built in 1870).

he concluded by falling drunkenly from the platform into his audience's midst. A dim view was taken, however, of the old rascal's bouts with the bottle during the Fenian crisis of 1866. There was a change of attitude setting in and hardening.

By the 'eighties there were temperance groups meeting regularly near the heart of Yonge Street's drinking community. They met in what some of the merrier sparks of the town thought to be the aptly named Oddfellow's Hall at the Alice Street corner of Yonge; in the Wolseley Temperance Hall on the Gerrard Street corner; in the Albert Hall near the corner of Albert Street and Yonge; and in a building on the corner of Yonge and Louisa Streets.

A philanthropic but very profitable offshoot from the temperance cause were the coffee houses organized under the patronage of 'some of the best people in Toronto.' In 1881 the Toronto Coffee Association was formed with C.S. Gzowski as president. The first coffee house of the Association was opened in February, 1882.

And for any landlubber gullible enough to believe tales that a sly dram could be had by going aboard a steamer where drink was available as soon as the ship left the pier,—forget it. The steamers didn't ply the Lake for pleasure cruises on Sundays; a point often stressed in the advertisements. On top of that, during the navigation season the YMCA held a Bethel Service every Sunday evening on board the S.S. 'City of Toronto' at the Yonge Street wharf, for those in peril on the water or elsewhere.[30]

The YMCA was naturally very active in the temperance movement. They moved to a new building at Yonge and McGill Streets in 1887, and that staunch teetotaller, Senator John Macdonald, was at the dedication ceremony.

Temperance and religion joined to make a great racket for the cause of sobriety, with much support coming from the Methodist Church in which, ironically, several successful brewers were prominent. People were encouraged to take a pledge of abstinence, which was fair enough, but there was a zealous, fanatic fringe that wanted to have the sale of liquor drastically curtailed, abolished even.

And don't, whatever you do, stumble on the path to salvation. "John Dineen, who has taken the pledge several times and broken it, was found lying insensibly drunk, on Saturday, on Yonge street. He was fined $50 or 6 months."[31]

One staunch Methodist, whose business shook up Yonge Street, took his beliefs into the conduct of his store, where neither liquor nor tobacco was allowed, or even displayed.

Timothy Eaton, a clear-eyed, round-faced fellow with a restless jig-style look to him, came from Ballymena in Ireland and had little more than the bundle on his back when he came out to join his sister and brother in Canada. He started storekeeping at St. Mary's in 1860. He was therefore no greenhorn in the game when in 1869, he bought the Britannia House, a small store at the southwest corner of Yonge and Queen Streets. In the opinion of his contemporaries it was a thoroughly unfashionable spot to start a business.

There he candidly advertised with a message similar to that of John Macdonald's verse:

> EATON'S
> CHEAP
> STORE
> MAKE A NOTE OF IT

and offered his wares for 'Cash and One Price,' a flat charge openly stated, and no haggling. In his store a place would always be found for any of his countrymen out to make an honest way in North America.

He was an outstanding success and confounded more than just his commercial rivals. Old Bishop Strachan, the stalwart champion of Simcoe's ways, had died on the first day of November, 1867, in a time that saw the last dissolving vapours of Simcoe's Episcopal vision. Eaton was the embodiment of the triumph of the Methodists in the Toronto business world, and when his son became Sir John Eaton, an aristocracy undreamed of by Toronto's founders was accepted.

Mulvany may have written some pretty pompous stuff about business men, but the truth that he tried to expound was more aptly expressed in a later age by Sir Winston Churchill, 'business is the horse that pulls society's cart.'

Eaton's greatest rival followed in the tradition of Macdonald and Catto, the business doyens. Robert Simpson was another conscientious Scot who had come out to Canada at the same time as Catto and during 1858 to 1871 worked for a shop in Newmarket. At the beginning of 1872 he came to Toronto and opened a small and unremarkable dry goods store on the northwest corner of Yonge and Queen Streets. This was near the vacant lot south of Albert Street where the old Yonge Street omnibuses had been stored upon the closing of their service in 1861.

And it wasn't the choicest of spots, surrounded by other dry goods stores, oyster shops, confectioners and seed merchants. The Globe Hotel was just a few steps down the street. Beer, oysters and cry havoc; the corner at Queen was the gathering place for the lads of the village; perhaps a hangover from the days when it was the site of the old Rob Roy and Sun Hotels. Whatever the reason, the corner had changed vastly from the days in the 1820s when, according to Dr. Scadding, 'travellers got lost in the woods looking for a house' at the intersection of Yonge and Queen Streets.

The Daily Telegraph of September 7, 1870 described how, on the night before, "Police Sergeant Ward espied a crowd of rowdies collected on the corner of Yonge and Queen streets, many of whom, by a significant necktie, he recognized as 'Young Britons.'..." One of the mob refused to move on when so ordered and was promptly arrested and lodged in gaol.

When another fracas took place at the same spot in the following month, the newspaper announced that enough was enough, and that the authorities "should keep an eye after the batch of rogues who nightly assemble" at the corner with no good intentions toward themselves or anybody else.

The 'Young Britons' were a gang whose main pastime was trading blows with a rival brew of brawlers know as the 'Young Irishmen.' Their 'significant neckties' probably showed no more originality than being orange or green in colour. To say, however, that the 'Young Britons' were a branch of the Protestant Irish Orange organization brought loud howls of denial from the 'bhoys' of the Orange Lodges that, despite the Irish talent for disorganization, exerted no small force in the civic affairs of Toronto and in Ontario generally.

The Protestant versus Catholic bitterness had blended into the general scrapping of the 1830s when the Yonge and Queen corner had some notoriety as 'Rebels' Corner.' Near there had been the Toronto Foundry that under Norton's management had manufactured the canon which was not finished in time for delivery to W.L. Mackenzie's followers.

The northwest corner had been the site of the old Sun Hotel, built by Mackenzie's brother-in-law, John McIntosh. It was virtually the headquarters for "Wee Willie" himself, who couldn't organize anything, even a rebellion, and who was probably fortunate in abandoning his early trade of shopkeeping for politics.

What a change by the 'seventies: good, hardheaded, well-organized business at a spot where for long there had been sound and fury of one sort or another, but none of it signifying a great deal except to those making the noise.

Organization—that was perhaps the key word for Toronto generally in the 'sixties. The Police Force for one was much improved after 1859. It was no longer the muddy-booted, flatfooted-caricature like the Keystone Cops after Captain

W.S. Prince, late of the 71st Highland Regiment of Light Infantry, took over. As Chief of Police he introduced some discipline into what had been a collection of politically-controlled amateurs.

There was pressure from society and religion for orderliness and, above all, loyalty. John O'Brien, Daniel Scanlon, James Glynn and Francis Martin, being found guilty of "cursing Her Majesty the Queen," were each fined three dollars and costs and bound over to keep the peace.[32]

By that time, the era of the Sun Hotel was extinct. Elliot's Sun had successively become the Falcon, the Craven Heifer and finally Fuljames' Hotel before being destroyed by fire in 1855. From the ashes the eventual phoenix to emerge was Robert Simpson's store.

Despite the gloom and doom prophecies of the business world's Jeremiahs, the choice of Yonge and Queen was a good one for both Eaton and Simpson. Business boomed. In 1881 Simpson was able to move to a larger building south of Queen Street, and Eaton migrated to the northwest corner, taking over what was known as the Page Block, the stores of Gibbs, Page and Company. It must have been a fire-jinxed corner, because in 1895 Simpson's new store went up in flames, but it was quickly rebuilt. Other stores established a familiar name in their day, although none equalled the Eaton-Simpson duo for longevity.

The other main corner, at Yonge and King Streets, was known with simple distinction as 'The Corner.' It was dominated by the Ridouts, Aikenhead and Crombie on the northeast. On the southeast was the side entrance to John Kay's dry goods store, a branch of the well-known John Kay Carpet House at number 34 King Street West. John Kay was from the north of England and was the inventor of an automatic shuttle for carpet weaving. Moses Staunton's wallpaper warehouse was on the northwest corner. Across from Staunton's at number 7 King Street West, just off Yonge, was a stylish store for which those of Yonge Street were considered to be no sort of competition whatsoever; Fulton, Michie and Company.

Michie, another Aberdeen name, had started in May, 1835 with the sale of a hogshead of gin to a William Gilmore at three shillings and tenpence per gallon for the sixty-three gallons in the hogshead, and had not looked back since. In the 'sixties, George Michie also ran a store at the southeast corner of Yonge and Front Streets, across from the American Hotel.

By the mid-sixties, Fulton, Michie and Company were held to be without peer upon King Street. Their agents would scour Europe to search out choice delica-

1947

cies for their leisured, wealthy customers, while Yonge Street was still in the world of beer, biscuits and seeds. Like an old soldier, Michie's seemed merely to fade away when it was rather ironically absorbed by Simpson's in 1947.

Just north of "The Corner" was Dineens' the hatters, W. and D., where located "most of the best trade of the city centres" (in 1883).[33] Opposite Dineens', on the east side was Harry Piper's furnishings. Harry started Toronto's first zoo and became a city alderman. He was in the habit of taking cartloads of flowers to distribute among the ragged urchins in his district, the notorious St. John's Ward that was dubbed 'The Ward' in simple infamy. Piper Street was named after him.

Harry's father, old Noah, ran a store called, of all things, the 'Ark House' at number 169 Yonge Street, where he sold such assorted items as bird cages, baths, croquet sets and babies' prams.

While many of the dry goods people moved northward on Yonge Street in the late 'sixties, the druggists bounced up and down the street like ping-pong balls. Shapter and Coombe started out together at the southeast corner of Yonge and Richmond Streets. In the 'sixties, Shapter migrated south to number 78 and

Grocers
Importers of
Teas, Wines
Liquors &c.

Jaffray & Ryan
244 Yonge Street.
c.1880.

Wines packed in hampers and "delivered free of charge
on board the cars in Toronto." (The Globe, 1885).

Coombe came to roost nearby at 104 while Harry Rose moved into their old premises to start his drug store.

In 1870, Burden and Pearson succeeded Coombe at 104, and by 1876 Harry Rose had set himself up at the southeast corner of Yonge and Queen Streets, across from Eaton's and Simpson's. Neil Love then took over the old Yonge and Richmond drug store. At the same time Shapter headed north again, and on the northeast corner of Yonge and Carlton Streets, at number 443, Shapter and Jeffreys were in business as druggists.

The first Jewish congregation in Toronto, founded in 1856 and called the Sons of Israel of the City of Toronto, worshipped for twenty years in a room over Shapter and Coombe's old Yonge and Richmond drug store.

At this stage of the game there was also some sort of competition for Michie's from Thomas Griffiths on the south corner of Albert Street. A grocer and wine merchant dealing in teas and coffees, he advertised himself as a 'London and Italian' warehouseman.[34] It was usual for the high-class grocer of those days to describe himself as an 'Italian warehouseman,' thereby indicating that he dealt in wares superior to the mundane necessities of daily existence.

A similar store was Jaffray and Ryan's, grocers and importers of teas, wines and liquors, at Yonge and Louisa Streets. Mulvany in his exuberance described the store as having "a reputation second to none in the Queen City of the West."[35] An opinion which Mulvany neither explains nor justifies.

At least stores such as Griffiths' and Jaffray's drove a wedge of civilization between the bilious beer-and-oysters mob and the temperance fanatics, the soda-water ascetics.

At the end of the 'sixties James Eves had owned a soda-water manufactory at number 107 Yonge Street, on the east side near the Adelaide corner. Shortly after that he abandoned his business to become a great worker for the Salvation Army whose members tried methods more effective than prohibition for the victims of drink.

Temperance meetings and hymn-singing didn't do much for those with hangovers. In those days before bromo-seltzers and aspirin the 'cure' was often digestive aids, or 'stomachics' as they were known. On the west side of Yonge Street in the 'sixties, just below Elm Street, was the manufactory of William Moore, the inven-

1878 - The red brick store of I. & H. Cooper on the s/e corner of Yonge and Adelaide Streets.

1900-1905 - The business office of the TORONTO STAR.

The Toronto News Company – 42 Yonge Street – c. 1881.

tor and purveyor of a stomachic concoction known as Stoughton Bitters. It certainly did not reach the popularity of Lydia Pinkham's Vegetable Compound as a saviour of the human race, and soon vanished from the street.

One would-be, and anonymous benefactor to victims of loose habits had an unintentionally funny advertisement for "YOUNG MEN—THE GREATEST Medicine to the World—Certain and speedy cure of weakness and debility of sexual organs, arising from bad habits of youth. No cure, no charge."[36] This nameless quack, or perhaps a discreet lady of pleasure, operated from number 411 Yonge Street at Carlton. An interesting address, because the Toronto Directory of the time lists the occupant as a Miss Christina Wilson. Across Carlton Street, however, at 443 Yonge was Isaac Lewis, druggist, soon to be succeeded by the well-known Shapter and his partner Jeffreys.

Other names well-known to the shoppers of the day were Meakin's dry goods, first at 181 then at 348 Yonge Street; E.&C. Pearson's across from Jaffray the grocer; M.&W. Pearson's dry goods, still at number 158, the old 'Large 103' of John Macdonald; Bilton's fish and game store at 188, just above Queen Street.

James W. Gale was long established at the southwest corner of Yonge and Adelaide Streets, where he ran a 'shirt factory' and supplied paper collars. His tailor's shop, however, was on the more fashionable corner of King and Bay Streets. "Gale's shops—Dress goods—Parasols and Sunshades—Nottingham lace curtains."[37]

The sign of a bear marked the premises of J.&J. Lugsdin, hatters and furriers at number 101 Yonge Street. Perry the hatter was under the sign of the Big Hat at

121, where he had moved in 1872 from 31 King Street West. An indication that Yonge Street was coming up in the world.

When the dry goods business had been in its infancy, the firm of McMurrich and Company shifted from King Street to 34 Yonge Street in 1832 where it stayed for many years. During this time, McMurrich family members played a prominent part in the city's affairs. Nearby, just above Wellington Street, was the wholesale dry goods business of John Robertson, the father of J. Ross Robertson who started the *Daily Telegraph*, later the *Telegram*. In the 'forties, the dry goods store of the highly successful William McMaster had been next to Robertson's, but it made way for a block that became the Dominion Bank building in the 'eighties.

J. Ross Robertson's *Evening Telegram* offices were on the east side of Yonge Street just below King from mid-1876 until 1881 when they were moved to the corner of King and Bay Streets. The rival newspaper, *The Globe*, was in offices on the southwest corner of Yonge and Melinda in the early 'nineties, but the building was destroyed by the fire of 1895.

Yonge Street in the 'seventies and 'eighties fast developed an air of solemn respectability. True, there was not much uniformity. It was still a clutter of buildings, some of brick and wood, some of stone, solid and well-made, others of aging wood sagging into a bulgy, despondent middle-age.

To tone things up, there were the banks. By 1884 these were: the Bank of British North America on the northeast corner of Yonge and Wellington; the Bank of Montreal's splendid structure on the northwest corner of Yonge and Front; the Central Bank on the east side of Yonge north of Wellington; the Canadian Bank of Commerce on the south corner of Colborne, a street unflatteringly described as "narrow, dirty and gloomy."[38] Both Front and Wellington Streets had 'imposing buildings.' And at 'The Corner's' southwest side was the Dominion Bank building.

Here Elias Rogers, a prosperous young coal and wood merchant, had his head office. He had opened an office in Toronto in 1876 in partnership with F.C. Dinniny of Elmira, New York. They made their fortune from interests in Pennsylvania coalfields, from where ships brought in cargoes directly to the Toronto waterfront in the 'eighties. Rogers had his coal yard at the Esplanade and Princess Street and a branch office at 418 Yonge Street. P. Burns, another coal merchant, had his yard at the Yonge Street wharf and his office at number 390. Elias Rogers

Bank of Montreal (built 1885) – N·W Corner, Yonge and Front Streets

was descended from one of the early settlers, the pioneer Quakers who came up from Pennsylvania to Newmarket at the start of the nineteenth century.

The most ambitious effort on the street was the Arcade, for which the Bay Horse Hotel had been knocked down. Standing between Yonge and Victoria Streets, it was opened in 1883, a veritable launching with an accompaniment of bands, bunting and flowers. Three stories high, with its vaulted iron frame and glass roof containing some one hundred shops, with ornamental iron crosswalks, balustrades and sweeping stairways, it looked as though a gigantic ocean liner had run aground on Yonge Street. Mulvany, with his usual unabashed bravura, claimed that it would be "what Burlington Arcade is to London, the Palais Royal to Paris, the haunt of fashionable loungers."[39]

Further refinements came in the form of restaurants. In 1872 the St. Charles Restaurant was opened at number 68-70, its proprietor Abner Brown. And in 1879, McConkey, who had started out with a confectioner's store, lit his restaurant with the first electric power generator in Toronto. By the 'nineties McConkey's on Yonge Street was at the head of the list of popular and fashionable restaurants.[40]

And Harry Webb, probably a connection of Tom Webb the confectioner, had a catering business and restaurant at number 447 Yonge Street. Harry was locally famous for the splendour of his wedding cakes.

For 'fashionable loungers,' however, King Street still held sway in Toronto. Its corner with Yonge Street was a busy intersection, the hub of city activity. *The Daily Telegraph* of December 5, 1870 reported that, "By actual count 689 vehicles passed the corner of Yonge and King streets between the hours of 9 o'clock a.m. and 5 o'clock p.m. on Saturday. An eccentric old gentleman, who posted himself at a window overlooking the corner, furnishes us with this interesting item."

Canon Arthur Jarvis, grandson of Lieutenant Colonel Stephen Jarvis who was second cousin to Simcoe's Secretary Jarvis, recalling his student days in the 'seventies, said that promenading King Street was then quite a feature of Toronto's social scene.[41] Those who followed Oscar Wilde's dictum that "one should either be a work of art, or wear a work of art," displayed themselves on King Street.

One spectator of this parade was intrigued by seeing "two young ladies about sixteen or seventeen years of age, each wearing a blue ribbon attached to her walking jacket, having the words, 'Flirtation Club Committee' printed thereon in small gold letters."[42] Desperate, if discreet measures, such as the young man who advertised in the personal columns that he wished to correspond with an unlimited number of young ladies, the object being fun.

While Canadians did not wish to see the strict chaperone system that was then in vogue in Europe, they felt that parents should be made to instill a greater sense of responsibility in their teenage children. Especially when old Mrs. Grundy was forever gleefully reporting young women 'of no good intentions' strolling on Yonge Street below Queen between seven and ten o'clock in the evening. A column in *The Globe* of October 21, 1882 commented at some length on the behaviour on the streets:

> Folly's Victims.
> ... Any one whose business leads him down Yonge or King street on
> a Saturday evening will know what we mean. He will there see
> young girls in their teens and out of them, who ought never to be
> seen on the streets of an evening without a protector, going about
> alone or with companions of their own kind, ogling the young
> fellows they meet, getting up flirtations with any whose attentions
> they can attract, and giggling like geese, instead of flushing with
> maidenly indignation at the jostling and other familiarities of
> young fellows they have never met before. These young fellows are

Fulton, Michie & C⁰   N.W. Corner, King & Yonge.

YONGE/KING 1866

sure to be anything but desirable companions, for if they had any
delicate instincts they would be repelled rather than attracted by
such demonstrations.

The newspapers passed on the latest tips in fashion to the King Street prowl-
ers, 'putting on the English' was the current slang for men in the height of style.
The latest thing in gentlemen's scarves was called 'Our Fritz,' with the 'Prince of
Teck' as popular as ever, but with the knot being made much larger than before.[43]

Women were advised that "the last ukase of fashion declares the chignon in all
its forms banished from her dominions. For which all thanks."[44] Like the colleen
in the garden where the praties grew.

Yonge Street wasn't with it. Two years after that tidbit of fashion and W.O.
Littleford was still advertising 'Chignons' at number 170 Yonge Street, as was
John Douglas at 219. George Ellis had 'human hair' chignons in his store at 179,

and perhaps the best-known and most exotic was at 105, where wigs and toupees could be bought at Dorenwend's Paris Hair Works. And to top it all off was the Dominion Chignon Manufacturing Company of J. Fawns at number 96 Yonge Street. These were in the decades of the 'seventies through the 'eighties.

By 1884 Yonge Street was well-established as a commercial thoroughfare in the city, as the following contemporary account shows:

> From the Esplanade to King Street [Yonge] is lined by handsome buildings, chiefly occupied as banks, insurance offices and whole-sale business houses, one of its most prominent features being the Custom House on the corner of Front. Above King, Yonge Street is not rich in architectural specimens, though here and there a lofty building of recent construction towers above its neighbours. Until, say, within the last ten years, the structures lining this portion of the thoroughfare were of the plainest description—mainly two story (sic) buildings of the ordinary brick-and-mortar or rough-cast type. But of late several handsome stores have been erected, nota-bly the Arcade, just finished, a row of retail stores just above Queen Street on the west side, and another row on the opposite side just below Wilton Avenue. Unpretentious as its buildings are, however, Yonge Street is no whit behind King Street as to the amount of business transacted—if it does not even surpass its more fashionable sister in this respect.[45]

Beyond a doubt, Dickens would have been impressed by that. It was a far cry indeed from what he had seen in 1842, and a vast improvement upon the hodge-podge of struggling businesses that straggled up from the wharf in 1860.

As the cool, green-shading trees and lanes made way for the increasing number of shops, so these must have become stifling in Toronto's roasting summers, the streets dusty and uncomfortable. The local rate for watering Yonge Street in 1870 from Bloor Street to the Davenport Road was two mills in the dollar.[46] Then, when the torrential spring rains made a bog of the place, people worried about disease-carrying waste being washed under the cedar-block paving and the sidewalks.

In winter, snow and ice discouraged shoppers and, as will be seen, led to dis-putes between shopkeepers and the city's transport authorities. A 'Daily Sufferer' complained to *The Globe* about the slippery condition of Yonge Street opposite Agnes (Dundas) Street. And the *Daily Telegraph*'s comic-character philosopher,

Josh Billings, said that, "One ov the hardest things for enny man to do, is tew fall down on the ice when it is wet, and then git up and praze the Lord."[47]

Complaints, complaints—the citizens of Toronto were forever griping about something. It was a civic hobby. If it wasn't the state of the streets, it was the transport system, or the conduct of the police. Given any occasion for a spectacle, however, and there was a great display of civic pride. On July 23, 1885, when the Queen's Own, the Royal Grenadiers and the Governor-General's Body Guard returned from service in the Northwest Rebellion, the city went wild:

> On Yonge Street the sight which met the eye was one which had never before been presented. Looking southward the view was beautiful. Arches, flags, banners, festoons of flowers and evergreens, with multitudes of spectators in windows and on housetops, as well as on the crowded thoroughfares, as street after street was passed, under arch after arch, formed a scene which could only again be repeated under like circumstances, and which will in all probability never occur. It was joyful, enthusiastic and loyal, and will live in the memory of all who witnessed it while life shall last.[48]

Like all pride, however, it was expansionist, and where Yonge Street was concerned, there was only one direction in which to expand—northward.

CHAPTER TWO

NORTHWARD GROWTH

1875-1914

I n spite of the imposing Customs House, the Bank of Montreal building and
the ambitious Arcade, style never came to Yonge Street. As the city inched a
predatory path northward, gorging and slowly digesting, Yonge Street grew
commercially, but it remained the same narrow, untidy, unplanned straggle of
shops that had marked its commercial beginning.

And in the city the street could only be described as sporadically residential
after the middle of the nineteenth century. By then the old duelling meadows and
orchards, the wagon makers and smiths, and the unpretentious houses were in
retreat before the advancing shops.

North of Maitland Street there was a brief stand by some fairly imposing
houses, sometimes described as 'country homes,' but surrounded not so much by
trees and rolling meadows as by the makers of farm implements and by assorted
widows' and tradesmen's unremarkable dwellings. Gentlemen's residences gave
only a passing nod to Yonge Street.

A Captain Stupart, late of the Royal Navy and employed by a firm of Lake
shipping underwriters, had a home just above Maitland Street in the 'fifties. It
was then the milieu of small tradesmen's premises and the widow Scanlon's mod-
est house, changing in the 'seventies to a medley of butchers, bakers and variety
stores. The most successful business there was George Pear's coffee and spice mills
at Alexander Street, where he made a considerable fortune. W.J. Smith owned
these mills in the 'seventies.

Two or three substantial houses, aloof like galleons in a fleet of galleys, gave evidence of their owners' commercial success in the city. Number 557 Yonge Street, at the corner of Wellesley, belonged to G.W. Dunn of Dunn and Company. At Yonge and Gloucester Streets stood the house built in 1848 for George Michie, founder of the flourishing grocery business. The most impressive number was 571, 'Dundonald,' after which the street is named. The house lasted into the 'nineties and had a varied history.

Built for a Mr. Proudfoot about the same time as George Michie's place, it was grandly named Kearsney House by its owner. Proudfoot was a grocer and wine merchant who had started out in the shop of D'Arcy Boulton, Jr., and subsequently had his own very successful business at the southwest corner of King and Frederick Streets. He was a director and president of the Bank of Upper Canada between 1835 and 1860.

In 1862 the Kearsney House passed to Mr. Robert Cassels, a Scot who was the chief cashier for the Bank of Upper Canada, and he in turn sold it in 1869 to Donald Mackay of the Gordon, Mackay dry goods company. It was then that the house got its name of 'Dundonald.'

It was a rather striking-looking house, being made of white bricks that most probably were manufactured from the clay deposits at the Eglinton brick works. That arch-aesthete, Oscar Wilde, would have approved of it. When he visited Toronto in the 'eighties he had expressed a marked preference for the use of white brick in buildings.

Apart from this rare little group of fairly fashionable homes there was little beyond Gloucester Street up to Isabella in the late 'seventies but vacant lots and Hy Doane's livery and cab stables. As R.L. Stevenson wrote, "there are no more meadows," only a road running straight and narrow toward the dust-hazed trees lining its dapple-grey cut through the northern suburbs and farmlands to the shining waters of Lake Simcoe beyond.

Until 1883 the city limits were at Bloor Street, immediately beyond which lay the village of Yorkville, the late Mr. Bloor's creation. The north borderland of Toronto between Isabella and Bloor Streets was a frontier edge of coal and wood merchants, the York and the Rising Sun hotels, Davis the horse-shoer, Dunlop the tinsmith and Schnurr the sausage-maker.

And there was the stubborn, ramshackle remnant from the pioneer days, the Gardener's Arms. In the last years of the nineteenth century its lease was taken over by a Mr. Graham who set up a blacksmith's business there. He became the

The Gardener's Arms — 1922 from a photograph in the STAR WEEKLY, 15 July, 1922.

The old Gardener's Arms #665–669 Yonge Street c.1890.

last of the "smiths between the waterfront and Thornhill."[49] When he started in business there, as many as thirty-one horses had been shod in a day, but toward the end of his tenancy in the 1920s, he was lucky to see twenty-five horses in a week.

He set up his forge in the former bar-room, and during his renovations old pennies that were dated earlier than 1800 and a George the Fourth shilling, tokens of more riotous days, came to light. The old dining room collapsed early in the 1900s, but in the yard were still the water troughs for stage horses and the pens for gaming cocks, a relic indeed.

And just within the bounds of Yorkville, standing guard for the old memories of Muddy York was the Red Lion Inn on the northeast corner of Yonge and Bloor Streets, scene of bygone election battles that had featured William Lyon Mackenzie and his following of Yonge Street farmers. In its heyday proprietors had advertised, 'the best strong beer at eight pence a gallon, New York currency, if drunk in the house.' When the place was finally deprived of its license as part of the effort to limit drinking in 1880, the days of the great drinkers were little more than a memory, or else grim examples for the propaganda of the Temperance societies.

Yorkville itself was a bastion that soon would crumble before the battering ram of progress, in this case transportation bringing the blessings and curses of civilization. The boundaries of settlement in the city had reached Bloor Street in the 'fifties, and from then it was only a matter of time before the Yorkville residents succumbed to the spider-lure of Toronto. In April, 1880, on the question of what was called the 'annexation' of Yorkville to the city, the village's voting was even.

One of the men most responsible for the improvement of city transportation was a resident of the suburb of Yorkville, Alexander Easton, an Englishman by way of Philadelphia. With the Englishman's sometimes eccentric enthusiasm for novelties, Easton was taken with the streetcars that were then being run in the United States, and he obtained from the city a license to operate a street railway. Thanks to his efforts, Yonge Street had the first horse-drawn streetcar line in Canada. It was opened on September 10, 1861, running on Yonge Street between King and Bloor.

The line was started with great fanfare as the first car, after several delays, moved down Yonge Street with an Artillery band playing jerkily on the roof, a polka would have made an appropriate tune. On the way south from Yorkville town hall the car went off the rails at Bloor Street, the city boundary. The first of a few derailments. The band and event-excited passengers would pile out to lift the car back on to its tracks, and by this off-again, on-again process the journey to St. Lawrence Hall was completed. The Yonge Street horse-car line was in business.

Mrs. John Catto, the wife of the successful dry goods storekeeper and linen merchant, could remember "The appearance of the first horse cars on Yonge Street. They were drawn by two horses and the fare was five cents. One line started at the St. Lawrence market and ran along King and up Yonge Street as far as the Yorkville town hall. Another line went up Yonge Street to Queen and went along Queen to the asylum. They only ran every half-hour."[50]

The new line ended the old omnibus service that had been operated in the city since 1849. Someone with the appropriate name of Shuttleworth had had a line on Yonge Street as far as Richmond Hill in 1847. The credit, however, for developing the first compact, passenger-service vehicle for transportation in Toronto goes to Henry Burt Williams, an enterprising cabinet-maker. His trade would explain the rather stylish, scrolled coach-bodies of the four six-passenger omnibuses with which he started his line to Yorkville in 1849. This line was superseded by Easton's horse-car railroad by an act of Parliament sanctioned on May 21, 1861.

As happens to the often worthwhile whims of Englishmen that are not put into practice forcefully enough, Easton's venture was not a paying proposition. His scheme flopped financially, and in 1869 an act for its relief was passed. The Toronto Street Railway was then sold to new owners, William T. and George Washington Kiely, who incorporated a new company, but with the old name, in 1870. Yankee know-how then made the system tick.

It may have been a going concern after that, but the method of operation brought howls from irate citizens who felt that the Company was getting too much of a good thing. The only revenue coming to the city was an annual tax of five dollars on each car owned by the Company. On January 27, 1875, *The Globe* got into the act with an editorial that loosed a blast at the

TORONTO STREET RAILWAY
... Our Commissioner brings up before the Police Magistrate house-holders who neglect to clear away the snow from before their doors. And he is quite right in doing so. We only wish he would extend his operations and pull up two or three times more than he at all troubles. Sure we are that any informer could easily find doz-ens of houses, on our greatest thoroughfares, from before which the snow has not all this winter been even once removed. But while householders are fined, the great offender—the Street Railway Company— goes scot free. To suit its own convenience and profit, that company has throughout all this season persistently kept to wheeled vehicles, and thereby made such deep ruts in the snow that there is no possibility of a sleigh or cutter crossing without a imminent danger of being overset. The whole centre of the streets is in this way practically reserved for the Company. ...

We Torontonians are a long suffering people. The wrong-doer has only to put a bold face on it, and persist in his iniquity, to be left 'master of the situation'.

Long suffering, perhaps, but in February, 1881 there was a battle royal between the Street Railway employees and the Toronto storekeepers along the Yonge Street route. The trouble was caused by the snow ploughs that were carried on the cars. They piled the snow to either side of the track, making the road impass-able for other vehicles. This obviously didn't do very much for business on the street, so the shophands were turned out to shovel the snow back on the tracks.

The Battle of Yonge Street, – February 1881.   from a drawing in the Canadian Illustrated News, 12 February, 1881.

As a result, the cars were blockaded by the mounds of snow, about a dozen being completely put out of action. The pubic, generally, was delighted.

It was the usual Toronto love-hate affair with its pubic services. In a city whose god was business, the suspicions of Seneca, like some ghostwriting on the wall, needled the public mind into uneasy awareness—was the great Toronto public being 'ripped-off' by the businessmen who operated its services? This came to the fore especially after 1881 when Senator Frank Smith gained control of the Toronto Street Railway. Whenever it was felt that authority was becoming high-handed, the public opposition was considerable.

Such was the case in 1886, when Toronto followed the lead of New York, where a strike of streetcar drivers had taken place on February 24. Feelings had run high between the pro- and anti-union factions and the New York police had intervened forcibly.

Unions were still something of a novelty at that time. Toronto in the 1870s was one of the first Canadian cities where the separate trades' unions came together in local assemblies so that labour interests might be united with a stronger voice for action. The most prominent grouping was a so-called secret society, the Noble and Holy Order of the Knights of Labour of North America that was very active in the 'eighties. To paraphrase Voltaire's comment on the Holy Roman Empire, the Knights were probably neither Noble, Holy nor an Order, but they remained a powerful force in Canadian Labour until the 'nineties.

Businessmen felt that unions would wreck Toronto's prosperity and strongly resisted the attempts to organize labour, even W.L. Mackenzie, ardent though he was for reform, had felt that unions would be damaging to production. In 1872 there had been stiff opposition to the '9 Hour Movement' to bring in a nine-hour working day. Those who had been successful in the rags-to-riches groceries and dry goods derby were convinced that they had made it without any favours and maintained the attitude that those who hadn't made it were jealous, lazy bums— go cry to somebody else was the attitude.

That attitude was typical of Senator Frank Smith, who prided himself on being 'a tough old nut to crack.' A native of County Armagh in Ireland, he had arrived in Canada at the age of ten, poorer than Murphy's potato patch, but determined to sprout like Jack's beanstalk as soon as he could take root. After farming near Toronto he went into the wine and grocery wholesale business in London where he became Mayor in 1866. He moved back to Toronto in the following year.

There was a commotion in 1870, when "the rumour [was] again revived that Frank Smith [was] to be made Senator; but there had been such a hue and cry about subservience to Roman dictation that Sir John [hesitated]."[51] Triumphing as usual, 'purty rich and mighty sly,' Smith became the only Roman Catholic to be appointed to the Senate by Sir John A. Macdonald in 1871.

By 1876 Smith was on the Board of the Toronto Savings Bank, and was at some time President of the Northern Railway. In 1881 he purchased a controlling interest in the Toronto Street Railway, which he then dominated in a splendidly dictatorial fashion that dynamited any happy nonsense that Mulvany chose to write about democracy in good old Toronto.

Once in control of the street railway, Smith, true to his beliefs and style, de-creed that no employee of the TSR would become a member of a union. Unions, in Smith's opinion, were a bad thing. It was no surprise, therefore, in March,

1886 when the TSR fired some employees who had defied Smith by joining the Knights of Labour.

On March 11, between three and four hundred employees of the TSR went on strike as a protest against Smith's dismissal of their co-workers. A few cars of the Company were run by non-union members during the early part of the day, but by three o'clock everything was at a standstill. The sympathy of the public, who by that time generally felt that the TSR was somehow getting too much of a good thing at the people's expense, was for the most part on the side of the strikers. In addition to the sympathizers, of course, there were the usual mobs that turned out in the hopes of some excitement.

They got it. Most of the crowd was gathered at Yonge and King Streets, while the TSR strikers and union members had collected at the Knights of Labour headquarters in the Arcade on Yonge Street. The crowd unhitched the horses from some of the cars, one of which was then gleefully pushed down Yonge Street by a gang of rowdies until it piled up in a snowbank. The opportunity for a street ruction was too good to be missed.

On Friday the twelfth, however, the police intervened. TSR cars were run with policemen on board to discourage any hooliganism and violence, but one of the cars ran into a crowd on Yonge Street and mud was thrown at it. A second car was then sent up the street with reinforcements and the police made a baton charge that got rid of the crowd in short order. The somewhat battered and muddied cars were then taken to the large TSR car-barns at the east end of Yorkville Avenue.

The offices of the TSR were on the ground floor of St. Paul's Hall that had been Yorkville's town hall before the village's absorption by Toronto. When the cars reached the Yorkville end of their run it was the practice to unhitch the 'up-bound' pair of horses that would then be led to the stables next to the barns. A fresh pair was walked over to Yonge Street and harnessed for the 'downbound' run.

During the Smith-Unions hassle the union-affiliated former employees of the TSR tried to set up a rival streetcar business of their own, but when their improvised stables were destroyed by fire in June the attempt was given up. As could have been expected, Smith was the eventual winner in the battle of Yonge Street, to reign supreme for a few more years.

The newspapers, the *Telegram* and *The Mail*, were critical of Smith, but *The Christian Guardian*, no doubt bearing in mind the prominence of many Methodists in business circles, hedged skilfully on the issues raised by the strike:

We think, therefore, that the Company went beyond its province
in discharging the men for joining a labour society. ... On the other
hand, if the complete mastery of the situation is in the hands of
large combinations of irritated workmen with strong class feelings,
and backed by the idle and unscrupulous of the community, the
decision is no more likely to be just.[52]

This did not offer any solution, but it was probably one of the best-balanced
summaries of the situation.

For the most part the public was not happy, being left with no alternative to
the somewhat uncomfortable, and unnecessarily so, TSR cars. And there seemed
to be no way of cracking that 'tough old nut,' Smith. When the city billed the
Company in 1886 for the cost of maintaining the paving along the horse-car rails
on Yonge Street, Smith flatly refused to pay up.

Eventually, however, the jig was up. The Kiely franchise was due to end in
1891, and with Smith's performance in mind, there were many people who
wanted to see public ownership of the street railway. City Council did not share
this particular enthusiasm and after much speech-making, skulduggery and shilly-
shally, the franchise to operate the street railway for thirty years was given to
George Kiely and the astute but devious railroad promoter, William Mackenzie,
later of the Canadian Northern Railway's Mackenzie and Mann fame. The franchise was signed on the first of September, 1891 and its terms were much tighter
than those of its predecessor. There was a fixed annual rental to cover street-
paving costs and the horses were to be replaced by electricity within three years.

The speed limit for the TSR cars had been a stately six miles per hour, but that
would soon be doubled and fairly dependable, regular schedules would put new
life into the push north; "a high economic status district expanded along Yonge
Street subsequent to the building of the Street Railway."[53]

The streetcar really made suburbia possible as improved service would allow
people to live outside the city limits and come in daily to their work. Electric
lines would speed up that process and aggravate the 'northern itch.'

For those wanting to travel out beyond the city limits, the old-reliable, omnibus-
stagecoach continued to be the usual way until the 'nineties, posting between
the long-established staging hotels and inns.

In the 'sixties, the stages would roll away from the Green Bush at four o'clock
every afternoon but Sundays, heading up Yonge Street to Hogg's Hollow at York

Mills. The old English currency found below the planks in the Gardener's Arms had, since 1858, been slowly replaced by the dollar and the fare to York Mills was twenty cents. From the Bay Horse Inn to Thornhill it was thirty-seven and a half cents.

During the 'seventies an omnibus would leave the Palmer House, the old Stage Hotel in Richmond Hill, at half-past seven in the morning for Toronto and would return from the Bay Horse Inn at half-past three in the afternoon:

> The Palmer House,
> RICHMOND HILL
> JOHN PALMER, Proprietor
> Having recently built the above House on the site of the old Stage Hotel, and furnished it throughout in first-class style, I am pre-pared to give the public the best of accommodations. Good sta-bling and attentive hostlers. Sample Rooms for Commercial Trav-ellers. Terms. $1 per day. The Richmond Hill Omnibus leaves this House at 7.30 a.m., for Toronto, and leaves Toronto at 3.30 p.m.[54]

The fare was by then fifty cents each way and if you missed the 'bus, too bad, because it only ran once a day.

There were no railway connections in Richmond Hill itself, but the Northern Railroad line went through Maple four miles to the west of the village and offered the only alternative public transport if the 'bus was missed. To catch the trains, W. Proctor of the Dominion Hotel started a stage line in July, 1878. Proctor's omnibus would leave the Cosgroves' Robin Hood Hotel in Richmond Hill at half-past seven in the morning and at one o'clock, quarter-past four and quarter-past seven in the afternoon and evening to meet the NRR trains going north and south.[55]

In 1899, Proctor's stage was still going from the Palmer House to connect with the mail and express trains. By 1900 the advertisements for Proctor no longer appeared. Improved systems of transportation had made the service unnecessary.[56]

In Thornhill, Bill and Tom Cook of the Yorkshire House had run the omnibus line that carried the mail from Toronto as far as the village, then they sold the business to John Thompson at the end of the 'seventies. John Thompson's Yonge Street Omnibus Service became perhaps one of the best-known outfits with a two-horse vehicle between Richmond Hill and Thornhill and a larger, four-horse stagecoach between Thornhill and Toronto. They ran until the last gasp of the stage route in 1896, when the radial street railway put it out of business.

John Thompson's omnibus outside the Dominion House Hotel on the east side of Yonge Street in Richmond Hill, c. 1895.

A small item in *The Liberal* of February 4, 1897 underlined the demise of the Thompson 'bus line. "The citizens of this village, [Richmond Hill] and all along Yonge Street will be glad to know that the Metropolitan Railway Company have employed Mr. R. Thompson, late of Thompson's bus line, to look after their parcels and all kinds of freight to or from the city. There has been considerable trouble and annoyance during the past few weeks over parcel delivery. ..." Thompson, it was assumed, would soon make delivery prompt.

He can't have provided all the answers, because in November, 1898 Levi Gaby advertised his 'Express' going to Toronto and back on Mondays, Wednesdays and Fridays. It delivered and collected parcels and freight and also delivered coal from Toronto, but seems to have been a very short-lived service.

John Langstaff, who owned the Hawthorn Mineral Springs on Benjamin Thorne's old property in Thornhill, had a favourite, unfinished tale connected with the Thornhill stage. A local young man called William Smith, finding little excitement in the life around him, had gone off one morning in the early 'sixties on Cook's stage to Toronto. From there he continued on to New York and enlisted in the 25th New York Regiment. In America's Civil War he found his sought-for excitement in action during the fighting near New Orleans and that was the last that was ever heard of him. Somewhere, probably, there is the grave of 'a Union Soldier' who was, in fact, one of the several Canadian youths who had gone out to find adventure in another nation's war.

The United States in those days seemed to provide better opportunities and held more dramatic appeal for restless youth than did Canada. America had an ebullient, roistering image. The legendary, great American cry of 'the mails must get through,' however, must have died out somewhere along the shores of the Great Lakes. Even from its earliest days the Canadian mail seems to have been one of the national games of chance.

The *York Herald* of May 22, 1879 carried a story of the mail stage on the way from Barrie to Penetanguishene. At that time the stage went from Barrie through Oro Township to Orillia and then on to Penetanguishene. The driver on this particular journey may have over-fortified himself against the elements, although the old, two-storey, white pine Last Chance tavern, the last before leaving Barrie, had by 1860 become the Green Bush Hotel and lost its license to sell liquor. In any event, the driver fell asleep soon after leaving Barrie.

He was awakened by a farmer's wife who was his passenger shouting, "I say, mister, if yees don't jump from that thar perch mighty quick you'll lose your coat-tails." The stage was on fire. The horses were unhitched with the assistance from the lady, but some of the mail was burnt. And the best advice offered by the newspaper was that, "In the meantime those who sent letters north by that mail would do well to duplicate them." It was obviously an at-your-own-risk service.

As such it didn't sit well with Canadians who had very much of a 'Polly-wants-a-cracker-right-now' attitude to their public services, after the fashion of impatient Americans. It was hoped that the railway would be much more efficient and reliable.

At the time of the mail-stage story just related, in 1879, the Northern Rail Road had put through a line at long last from Barrie to Penetanguishene—the same year that the Northern took over the Hamilton and Northwestern Railway with its line from Hamilton to Barrie and Midland. A good northern line, hope-

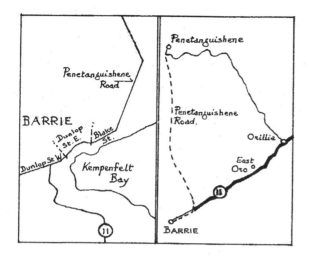

fully, would solve such problems as erratic mail and parcel services. As R.L. Stevenson said in *Virginibus Puerisque*, however, "Hope lives on ignorance."

An example of the unrelieved irritation with the Northern Railway can be seen in the *York Herald* of November 3, 1887 in an article rather sardonically styled "Enterprise—The mail from Toronto reached here [Richmond Hill] near noon on Tuesday last, having been detained waiting at the station for the down train which had got off the track up north. Think of it for a moment, the Toronto papers not reaching here, a place sixteen miles from the city, until nearly noon. We think some arrangement should be made to bring the letters and papers up the street. They should reach here at least by 9 a.m. On Monday, parties who left by the noon stage to catch the train for Toronto returned, after waiting at the station until 3 o'clock for the train from the north, it having met with an accident, got off the track or something else."

For the disgruntled and the disenchanted, hope was now transferred to the possibilities of another novelty, the electric streetcar, although the sceptics doubted its ability to climb the steep hills on Yonge Street north of the city limits.

By the time of the village of Yorkville's incorporation into the city of Toronto on February 5, 1883, the possibility of electric streetcars was coming rapidly close to being a fact.

In 1877 a Metropolitan Street Railway had been incorporated for the purpose of providing a horse-car service that would run north on Yonge Street from Yorkville to the town hall in the village of Eglinton. It was not until 1884, however, after Yorkville's annexation by Toronto, that the MSR started to use the franchise that had been granted to it. A single horse-car track was laid from a point just south of Summerhill Avenue to the Eglinton town hall at Yonge Street and Montgomery Avenue. The iron probe was reaching to a greater suburbia.

Mulvany, writing in the year of Yorkville's absorption into the larger fold, said that the village was a popular choice of location for those who wanted to live at cheaper than "downtown" housing prices, but needed easy street-car travel to their work in the city's core.[57]

As a place to live, Yorkville offered pleasant surroundings through the 'nineties and into the next decade of the twenti-eth century. Its quiet streets, cool and shady, made a wel-come relief from the hot and dusty city, although the iron grooves of advancing Toronto would gradually change that character.

Long gone, since 1865, had been the military Blockhouse in Yorkville, built in 1838 on

St. Paul's Hall,
Yorkville Town Hall,   destroyed by fire, November, 1941
(Clock installed in 1889)   demolished, May, 1942.

Yonge Street at Belmont to guard against a repeat of the 1837 march upon the city from the north. If anything, the march was now going the opposite way.

The quaint old Red Lion Inn, successively clap-boarded, stuccoed and painted white, soon succumbed in the late 'eighties with its bar room suffering the final indignity of becoming a flour and feed store.

Once annexed, Yorkville became St. Paul's Ward in recognition of St. Paul's Hall, Yorkville's rather bizarre-looking town hall that was on the west side of Yonge Street between Yorkville Avenue and Davenport Road. It stood in the centre of what had been Toronto's old Potter's Field, last resting place of the indi-gent, criminal and disgraced.

The hall was the village symbol, made of bricks from the blue clay of Blue Hill on the north side of the nearby Rosedale Ravine. Set over the circular window in the front of the building was Yorkville's peculiar crest. This was carved in stone and showed a barrel, a brick-mould, a jackplane and an anvil grouped about a central sheep's head. Against each of these signs was an initial to indicate the names of the five Yorkville councillors when the hall was built.

For obvious reasons that irked the temperance fanatics, the best-remembered of the signs was the beer barrel with the letter 'S' beside it. John Severn had started the Yorkville Brewery in 1832 at number 815-819 Yonge Street and during the 'eighties it was being run by his son, George. It was estimated that some two hundred thousand gallons were brewed there annually, until the place slowly folded by the 'nineties. The ruins were still there in the 1920s.

The brewery made a picturesque huddle of buildings, mellowed and irregular and appropriate to Yorkville, its eastern edge bordering on the old millpond that had been the source of power for Bloor's successful brewery. Severn, however, did not use water-power, but relied upon steam to drive his grinding mills. A sloping walkway ran from Yonge Street into the Yorkville Brewery and is remembered today in the name of Severn Street. Another street named after another brewer! Let John Graves Simcoe shudder.

An even more democratic thoroughfare is the present Hazelton Avenue, honouring old Joe Hazelton, a village worthy of the early 'sixties. Joe owned a one-horse cab. By hard work and careful habits he was said to have made over one hundred thousand dollars that were left to his widow and two sons. He was determined that his sons would be gentlemen. And the story went that he would al-

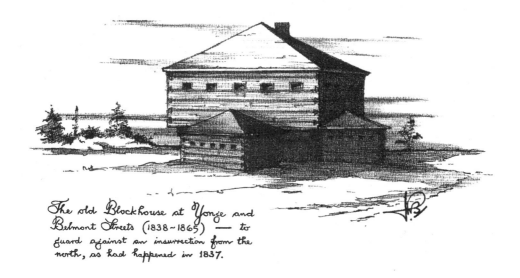

The old Blockhouse at Yonge and Belmont Streets (1838~1865) — to guard against an insurrection from the north, as had happened in 1837.

Yorkville's "curious," sculptured stone crest that was above the circular window in the old Town Hall. Surmounted by a beaver are the signs of a barrel, a brick mould, a jackplane and an anvil grouped about a central sheep's head. These, and the initials beside them, show the trades and names of the five Yorkville councillors when the Hall was built.
S – Severn, brewer   A – Atkinson, brickmaker.
W – Wallis, blacksmith   H – Hutty, butcher   D – Dobson, builder.

ways drive one of them to work, Joe on the box and the son riding inside the cab. Joe was the textbook example of how to get ahead by honest work, the argument to confound the improvident and the down-and-out.[58]

The village coroner in the 'seventies, Dr. Philbrick, was another well-known character. He lived on Yonge Street near St. Paul's Hall, opposite what was then Park Road, and if not slightly eccentric, he was at the least somewhat in advance of his day. When he and his wife separated, Philbrick kept their dog, to which he was greatly attached, However, an agreement was drawn up whereby his wife was allowed to visit the dog at stated times. The original case of 'love me, love my dog.'

Much of the village character remained through the 'nineties, its style that of Yonge Street in a more leisurely age. Photographs of Yorkville show an uncrowded stretch of irregular buildings along streets where Time seemed barely to stir the dust. There was even an apiarist, John McArthur, on Yonge Street at what was then Rosedale Lane.

Of the traditional village blacksmiths there were four, starting with C. Gaby on the east side of Yonge Street a few yards north of Bloor in the area where the Red Lion had stood. Near him, John Townsend had a livery stable and on the corner of the next street, Bismarck Avenue that became Asquith in the anti-German sentiment of the Great War, was the CPR Hotel run by Caspar Clark.

Above Park Road was the North Toronto Hotel and Dowden's smithy near the site of the defunct Severn brewery. Old George Severn still lived at number 849 Yonge Street, edged by the vacant lots above the street that perpetuated the Severn name. And northward from there was the typical outer suburban scene,

McLaren the blacksmith, Hall the tinsmith, lumber yards, vacant lots and private residences, with the Rosedale Hotel at Shaftesbury Avenue just below Summerhill, the city's limit on the east side of Yonge Street.

On the west side up to the limit at Farnham Avenue, the pattern was very much the same. The Boulton Meat Company was on the northwest corner of Bloor and Yonge Streets. To the north Haag's and Frogley's bakeries, Ford the butcher, Dobson's bookstore and post office and Shaw's grocery were grouped about St. Paul's Hall.

An indication of the coming change in the way of things was the Salvation Army's Industrial Home for Men above Davenport Road. And on the north and south sides of Frichot Street was a business better remembered as being at the Yonge and King corner a quarter of a century earlier, M. Staunton and Company, wallpaper manufacturers.

From there it was the outer fringe again: Albery's saddlery, Sheppard's brick-works, McQuain the carriage builder, small stores, vacant lots and private homes, up to Plowman the blacksmith and the residence of Edgar Walker, after whom Walker Avenue was named.

In 1897 the Canadian Bank of Commerce displaced Boulton's Meat Company on the northwest corner of Yonge and Bloor Streets, where it lasted until 1972, a

Bloor's Brewery, Rosedale Ravine ~ 1830~1875.   (from a watercolour by Paul Kane).
(The Yonge Street blockhouse at Belmont is on the skyline).

turreted bulk bolstering the confidence of the commerce-inspired buildings that gradually crowded and jostled the old town hall. In the 'nineties the latter provided the premises for the police station and for the Orange Hall. It subsequently became a firehall, and although swamped by the expanding city, it somehow survived, although very much altered, almost to the present day.

Beyond the edge of the older, more settled part of Yorkville, not far north of Belmont Street where the Blockhouse once had loomed with frontier-style authority, was the home of Senator Sir David Macpherson. The house stood near the southeast corner of Yonge Street and Macpherson Avenue that was named after him. The estate was called 'Chestnut Park,' its Yonge Street frontage having a line of horse-chestnut trees that would have done credit to the driveway of any English country house, or provided the proverbial shady spread for the village blacksmith. In this attractive residence and its setting, St. Andrew's College for boys was lodged from 1899 to 1905.

David Lewis Macpherson was a Highland Scot from Inverness who had about him more of the style of the fur-trading Scots than of those in Toronto's dry goods stores. In 1835 he arrived in Montreal to work in his elder brother's firm of Macpherson, Crane and Company that had a fleet of steamers and sailing vessels engaged in the forwarding trade, with connections in Quebec and Chicago.

He decided, however, that railways offered a more worthwhile business gamble and in 1853 he set out for Toronto and this greener field for speculation. In Toronto he joined forces with another enterprising developer, C.S. Gzowski, and they promoted the Port Huron to Detroit and London and the St. Mary's Railways.

Sir David is said to have been the owner of a brickworks in Toronto, but no evidence of its whereabouts could be found. Sir David became a director of Molson's Bank, the obvious result of his marriage to Elizabeth Sarah Molson of Montreal. Not for him the socially-cautious marriage advice culled from the shop-wisdom of his contemporary in the Senate, old dry goods John Macdonald of nearby Oaklands. It is not surprising that Macpherson became president of the prominent St. Andrew's Society in Toronto.

True to the fashion of a Highlander of his stripe, he was a Tory in his politics. In 1864 he contested with the Hon. John McMurrich to represent the Saugeen district in Parliament. McMurrich, from a farming family near Glasgow in Scotland, was of the dry goods persuasion, the well-established firm of Bryce, McMurrich with a store at 34 Yonge Street near Melinda in the 'sixties. Like a fair number of his fellow Lowland Scots, McMurrich leaned to the Reform, or Grit

1972 demolition of Canadian Imperial Bank of Commerce (built 1897)
N.W. Corner of Yonge & Bloor Streets (old site of Potter's Burying Ground.)

Party, and represented the staunchly Grit district of North York in the Ontario Assembly in 1867.

As for Sir David Macpherson, he became Speaker of the Senate in 1880 and was Minister of the Interior from 1883 to 1885, a job that led to his downfall. A government cutback in rations to the Indians of the North West, his lack of knowledge of that area and a consequent mishandling of events that ended in the 1885 Rebellion in the North West led to criticism that brought his retirement in that year. He was, without a doubt, on more solid ground when he rebuked the Hon. Richard Cartwright, the Minister of Finance, for remarks 'considered insulting to Highlanders'—for which he received an address in both English and Gaelic from the grateful Highlanders of the Glengarry community.[59]

'Chestnut Park' was a reflection of the Senator's position and style, being the most imposing of the country residences on that part of Yonge Street where the outriders of the city's settlement were climbing the hill to St. Clair Avenue in the 'nineties.

The northern boundary of the city, the old edge of Yorkville, became more blurred with each passing year as it was pushed across the no-man's land that lay between Yorkville and the area known as Deer Park. Never clearly defined as a district, Deer Park had not ever been officially incorporated, even as a village. As the city limit of Yorkville crept northward, so the southern line of Deer Park retreated. Contemporary writers avoided giving a finite edge to Yorkville, Mulvany loosely describing its northern demarcation as being the "city limits,"—no street names, no location to identify the line.

In the grey area of these vague boundaries stood the already mentioned 'Woodlawn,' the home of Judge Morrison on the west side of Yonge Street. When he died in 1886 a large part of the house, some two-thirds, was demolished, but the remaining portion is still lived in today at number 35 Woodlawn Avenue. At least it was more fortunate than the steamer that was christened 'J.C. Morrison' in recognition of the Honourable Justice's session as a president of the Northern Rail Road Company. The steamer burned to the waterline very shortly after being built.[60]

On the east side of Yonge Street and just north of 'Woodlawn' was another pleasant home, 'The Elms,' built by a John Rose who gave Rosehill Avenue its name. This was apparently the same John Rose who took over Joseph Bloor's old brewery and operated it for a brief time. The house was bought by Joseph Jackes of a well-known Toronto family and much later his son, E.H. Jackes, gave the name to Jackes Avenue south of Rosehill.

Across from the Jackes' house stood the first of the Yonge Street tollgates, originally at Bloor, then at Marlborough and finally at its Farnham Avenue location in 1870.

The tollgate was probably the traveller's best guide to the whereabouts of the city limits in the 'eighties. The identity of Deer Park itself was given the official nod when its post office was opened in 1878 near Benjamin Sinclair's grocery store that stood on the northeast corner of Yonge Street and St. Clair Avenue. The post office lasted there until some time in 1912.

Given the way that street names were tossed around in those days, it would be an obvious assumption that the ridged, gritty, tree-bordered pathway that was St. Clair Avenue owed its name to the owner of the corner grocery. Legends of the Clan Sinclair in Scotland attributed the family name to a Norman knight, Waldernus, Comte de St. Clair. Like most easy solutions, it was not the way that the avenue got its name if local stories are to be believed. Although the claim is not impossible, because there seems to be a fair degree of confusion over the origin of the name.

In the 1870s there were several market gardeners in the area of what was then known as the Third Concession Road. One of these characters, somebody called Grainger, is said to have prompted the use of the name St. Clair for the road, although why he chose it is not clear. The most common story was that 'St. Clair' was a nickname for Grainger in his youth, but it seems a pretty far-fetched sort of a yarn. Whatever the case, the Third Concession Road was being called St. Clair after 1878. A Grainger's nursery existed on Balmoral Avenue just off Yonge until the 1980s.

A traveller could probably more readily identify Deer Park by the presence of the inevitable corner inn, in this area it was the Deer Park Hotel on the southwest corner of St. Clair Avenue and Yonge Street. This was the spot where the lads of the village gathered, the community intelligence headquarters, best known as 'O'Halloran's,'—complete with village pump.

Looking across St. Clair Ave. at Yonge Street from the front of O'Halloran's Hotel on the s/w corner. Deer Park Presbyterian Church was on the n/w corner. (c. 1912).

The hotel was the usual two-storey, wooden job, built by Mike O'Halloran in 1862. He died in 1865 and the hotel was run for some years by D. Sellers until O'Halloran's son, also Mike, took over in 1878. It was demolished in 1924.

O'Halloran's would have made a grand place for that heart's-delight of the Irishman, the wake. Immediately to the south was St. Michael's cemetery with a Roman Catholic chapel and school, a typical village juxtaposition of the secular and sacred spirits, true to the 'in the midst of life we are in death' theme. Today, only the cemetery remains, a vast, departed regiment of Irish names: Kellys, Flynns and McBrides. It is reached by a narrow lane that runs between a Home Hardware store and Aida's Falafel.

If parts of Toronto had about them the air of a Little Dublin, Deer Park had some of the flavour of an Anglo-Irish fief in Kildare. The village forge was east of O'Halloran's on Pleasant Avenue, now Pleasant Boulevard. North of St. Clair Avenue were small farms, market gardens, the residences of a departed gentry and the sprouting homes of recently successful businessmen.

The forty acres of land that made up the estate of Deer Park from which the village took its name were part of a much larger Crown patent made out to Frederick, Baron de Hoen in 1802. The baron was a former Hessian officer who was given two hundred acres for his services to the British government and who set up a two-room log house where he farmed at the northwest corner of what became Yonge and Eglinton. Like many army officers, he was no great success at pioneer farming and was slowly bogged down in debts.[61]

To raise a financial wind, he sold off the south forty acres of his two hundred to the Elmsely family, from whom they were in turn bought by Agnes Heath in 1837. Mrs. Heath was the widow of an officer in the army of the Honourable East India Company, Colonel Heath, who had been killed in its service in India. The house that was built on the Heath estate was known as Deer Park, with grounds well rolled and trimmed in the English manner. The family name is perpetuated in Heath Street.

At some time the Heath estate was divided into lots, because in 1847 Mrs. Heath's son, Charles, sold five one-acre lots to an officer of the Royal Engineers, Colonel Arthur Carew. The Colonel built an attractive residence on his purchase and called it Lawton Park. It was locally renowned for its carefully landscaped grounds and secluded setting that was entered through lodge gates fronting on old Yonge Street, now Lawton Boulevard. The property contained a carriage house, dovecote, root house, vinery and potting sheds.

The house and grounds were sold to a John Fisken in 1850. The next home west of Fisken's was that of William Ramsay who, in partnership with Fisken, founded the Imperial Bank. Ramsay had a profitable wholesale grocery business at Front and Scott Streets and Fisken was a financial broker on Scott Street.

Shrewd business methods took the place of the squirely habits of the military gentry. Fisken bought the land on the east side of Yonge Street, between the south edge of Mount Pleasant cemetery and Clarence Avenue, now Heath Street East, running east to Bayview Avenue. He sold off the lots on this purchase and also built two houses that looked out on the east side of Yonge Street.[62]

One of these houses was bought by Elias Rogers who had done extremely well in his coal business, with a branch in Yorkville at number 793 Yonge Street in the 'nineties and, in the nineteen-hundreds, at number 1131 next to the CPR crossing. Fisken opened Glen Avenue to run east from Yonge Street, today it is called Glen Elm Avenue, and the Rogers' residence was named Glen House.

During the wave of enthusiasm for the Reform group in Toronto's 1887 municipal elections, Elias Rogers was boosted by the Reformers to run for mayor. This campaign soon flopped, however, when it was found that Rogers had been dealing with a cabal of coal merchants to fix the price of coal in Toronto. It was probably just as true to say then what is often said today, that most people live in Toronto to make money. But price fixing was a shade too sharp for politicians wanting to create the image of Toronto the Good and Rogers had to go.

Old Seneca's crack about those who chased after wealth had hit home this time. The successful candidate for mayor was the Irishman, E.F. Clarke, a Deputy Grand Master of the Orange Lodge and the editor of the *Sentinel and Protestant and Orange Advocate* that waged a continual war of words with George Brown's Liberal newspaper, *The Globe*. While politics provided the Irish with an outlet for their charm and wit and for their love of paradox, fighting and phrases, it was generally the Scots merchants who dominated the business and financial life of the Queen City and of Ontario. The Scots even set a social tone that was different from what might have resulted if Simcoe had been able to impose his English ways.

When St. Andrew's College was moved to a new location in North Rosedale in 1906, the president of the school's board of management was John Kay Macdonald. He was a prominent member of that Scots community and managing director of the Confederation Life Association. The pupil body in the school reflected something of the makeup of an English minor public school and of To-

RULES FOR STAFF
1878

1
Godliness, cleanliness and punctuality are the
necessities of a good business.

2
This firm has reduced the hours of work, and the clerical staff will now
only have to be present between the hours of 7 a.m. and 6 p.m. on weekdays.

3
Daily prayers will be held each morning in the main office.
The clerical staff will be present.

4
Clothing must be of a sober nature. The clerical staff will not disport
themselves in raiment of bright colours,
nor will they wear hose, unless in good repair.
Overshoes and topcoats may not be worn in the office,
but neck scarves and headwear may be worn in inclement weather.

5
A stove is provided for the benefit of clerical staff. Coal and wood must be
kept in the locker. It is recommended that each member of the clerical staff
bring four pounds of coal each day during the cold weather.

6
No member of the clerical staff may leave the room without permission from
Mr. Rogers. The calls of nature are permitted and clerical staff may use
the garden below the second gate. This area must be kept in good order.

7
No talking is allowed during business hours.

8
The craving of tobacco, wines or spirits is a human weakness,
and, as such, is forbidden to all members of the clerical staff.

9
The owners recognize the new Labour Laws, but will expect a great
rise in output of work to compensate for these near Utopian conditions.

Conditions of work laid down by Elias Rogers for his staff in 1878.

ronto society. The successful business class and the professional circles provided the majority of the school's students. There were the Dineen boys of the hatter family, John Kay Jnr. of the carpet firm, the Gooderham sons, hardware Piper's son Reginald, Joseph Ellsworth Flavelle, the meat baron's heir, young Albert Britnell and young Rufus of the Skinner family that had a grocery business on Yonge Street. Professor G.M. Wrong's sons and the sons of several medical men represented the professional strata. 'Old King Coal' Rogers sent his son, Clarence Elias, there in company with Sydney Ford Fisken of the nearby Lawton Park family.

The Fiskens sold Lawton Park for $25,390 in September, 1904. The new owner was a John J. Palmer, apparently a very wealthy individual, who changed the name of the house to Huntly Lodge after the town in Aberdeenshire, Scotland where his father-in-law was born. Obviously a character of clannish instincts, Palmer built a white brick home for his daughter, Mrs. Baird, on the Lodge grounds facing Heath Street and called it The Neuk.

The village of Deer Park where English gentry had created reminders of England's green and pleasant land was incorporated into the expanding city of Toronto in December, 1908.

By that time, the Toronto Street Railway line had not only been electrified, it had reached its northern terminus on the south shore of Lake Simcoe. The job was done as usual to the accompaniment of demands, complaints, political palaver and threats to strike, with a workable solution somehow coming out of all of this. Two companies were involved in the process, the Toronto Street Railway and the Metropolitan Street Railway.

The setup was slightly ludicrous from the start. Although the Mackenzie combine owned both outfits, their tracks did not join up. The franchise terms would not allow it. After the Mackenzie-Kiely takeover in 1891 the TSR was called the Toronto Railway Company, its track running from St. Lawrence Hall to a point just south of the CPR tracks that crossed Yonge Street below Summerhill Avenue. The MSR also lost the 'street' from its title in 1897 and in 1904 it was taken over also by Mackenzie. Its track started just north of the CPR tracks and less than a hundred feet separated it from the Toronto Railway's line. Every effort was made by Mackenzie's outfit, legal or otherwise, to link the two lines, but the connection was not accomplished until the Mackenzie franchise expired in 1921.

The surprising thing was that Mackenzie, the artful dodger, never found a way around the impasse. One story had it that an attempt was made in the dead of night to join the lines, but somebody blew the whistle on the plot and the work-gang was scattered before anything could be done. The matter of a franchise regulation had not stopped him elsewhere.

Mackenzie was at one time the owner of the splendid country residence of Benvenuto on the west side of Avenue Road opposite Senator Macdonald's Oaklands. As a convenience for himself he had the TSR's Avenue Road streetcar line extended beyond the city limits to St. Clair Avenue, although to do so was in opposition to the franchise. The extension was not only convenient, it also added considerably to the value of Benvenuto and the property around it. When it came to railways, Mackenzie had all of the Scotsman's golden touch.[63]

The first real push for an electric streetcar line came after a visit by the MSR's directors to Pittsburgh, Pennsylvania in 1889. Impressed by the electric cars that they had seen there, they decided to have the same type of service on their Yonge Street line. The old horse-car tracks, however, were not up to the demands of the new system, which had to wait until 1891 before the existing Yonge Street line north of the city limits was rebuilt and electrified. In 1891 the MSR's new electric line reached from north of the CPR tracks to Glengrove Avenue between Eglinton and Lawrence Avenues. The Toronto Railway Company started its electric streetcar service in the city during the summer of 1892.

The Metropolitan's electrified line reached York Mills, the horse-traveller's horror that was Hogg's Hollow, by May, 1895. And immediately, of course, there was an increase in the clamour for an electric car service to the villages that lay farther north on Yonge Street's partly tamed, untrimmed outreaches. The omnibus was obviously as doomed as the dinosaur, the stream railway hadn't come up to the hopes for it. And what was good enough for the city boys was good enough for the lads of the village,—Polly wanted a cracker right away.

Back in 1888, the *York Herald* described the determination, perhaps even the desperation, of the villages to have a railway of some description. Messrs. Fullerton, Cook and Wallace were to make application to both parliaments to incorporate what would be the East Toronto and Richmond Hill Railway Company. A double or single line of track was to run from a point on the Midland Railway or on the CPR line from Claremont to North Bay, to pass through or very close to Richmond Hill. From there it would go south to Toronto, running as close as possible to Yonge Street.[64] No records follow to say what the parliaments thought of it, but the scheme fizzled out.

The electric streetcar, however, offered much better prospects. *The Liberal* was not slow in playing up the advantages of the streetcar line when the MSR electrified its tracks in 1891 with the obvious intention of extending its service northward:

> The scheme [the electric street railway] proposed is a new venture. The company willing to undertake the contract is the pioneer electric street car company in the Dominion. It is the longest route intended to be traversed by electricity [from the northern limits of the city to Richmond Hill] projected by any company.

And:

> Hitherto the tendency of the floating population is to mass in Toronto. Merchants, officials, mechanics and labourers prefer suburban residences. We see this in the outspreading of the city east and west. Rapid transit along Yonge Street would help to draw population to the north as well, and promote settlement not only at Richmond Hill, but at Thornhill, Newtonbrook, Willowdale, Lansing and York Mills.[65]

That was in 1892. For some people these notions must have seemed to have about as much chance of success as populating the Arctic. Even in the suburbs close to the city, in the town of North Toronto that included the villages of Davisville and Eglinton, there was considerable dissatisfaction with the services for transportation. This led to the creation of the Toronto Steam Belt Line Railway, chartered in 1889.

Passing north up the Don Valley, the Belt Line came through Mount Pleasant cemetery and ran west along the south side of Merton Street in Davisville where there was a stop just east of Yonge. The track went over Yonge Street on a bridge and passed north of Upper Canada College to a stop at Eglinton Avenue, then continued west to the Humber Valley before turning south. The line was not a success, however, in spite of the Grand Trunk taking over the operation in 1892. After two more years of losses the Metropolitan Street Railway bought out the property.

For those people beyond the suburbs Belt Line loops were a sideshow, a diversion from the pressing desire to see a line run directly north. Some time in 1895, at a public meeting in Richmond Hill, it was remarked that in 1873 Richmond

Hill and Markham had been on practically the same footing, but by the 'nineties Richmond Hill was marking time because of the lack of any convenient railway connection. Something had to be done to draw people and business northward.[66] In July, 1895 the Richmond Hill Council was petitioned to submit a bylaw to the village to grant a bonus of $10,000 to the MSR to extend its electrified line to Richmond Hill.[67] The petition was signed by most of the freeholders above $1,000 assessment.

With that sort of encouragement, things began to move, although it was not until more than a year later that The Liberal of October 22, 1896 reported, with a quiet relish, that Mr. William Mackenzie had been seen taking dinner at the Dominion House in Richmond Hill. The laying of a single track from York Mills was begun on October 26, 1896 with some three to four hundred men being employed in the process. Plowing the road for the track proved to be a harder business than expected because of the stones and three men were needed to hold each plow.

The residents along the way were at least given something to argue about as they watched the progress of the track-laying gangs of Italian 'navvies'—the 'navigators' who put down the railroad lines in the nineteenth century. Teams of horses hauled the thirty-foot long, six hundred pound rails in batches of six from the nearest railway stations. Local oracles made the gloomy prophecy that the steep slopes on parts of Yonge Street would make it impossible for the cars to climb the smooth rail-tracks and so defeat the whole enterprise. Progress must have its Jeremiahs.

It must have been a bonus for the sages of gloom and doom when there was the threat of a strike just south of the village of Thornhill. A group of men was seen marching up the hill with a red flag to advertise their demand for an advance in wages. They were met by their superintendent who gave them an immediate raise from a dollar to a dollar and twenty-five cents a day. Satisfied, the gang gave three cheers for Mr. Wray, furled their flag and tramped back to work singing 'For He's a Jolly Good Fellow,'—or perhaps its Italian equivalent.[68] The work gangs put in a ten-hour day.

The opening, ceremonial run of the first car to Richmond Hill between nine and ten o'clock on the night of November 19, 1896 was not a smooth operation. The overhead wiring at the northern end had not been completed in time for the inaugural run, hence the triumphal car with the appropriate cargo of civic dignitaries was hauled north by the old-reliable horses. At the top of each hill, however, the horses would be unhitched and the car allowed to swoop downhill on its own momentum. Upon grinding to a halt it would be harnessed again to the horses, ready for the next hill-climb. Overall, however, the scheme had proved to be a success, the gaps in the overhead wires were but a slight snag and the Jeremiahs were discredited.

In 1897 the line reached Oak Ridges and Bond Lake where Williams Bond's hired man had been harassed by Indians a century earlier. In the 'nineties the hotel at Bond Lake was leased by the Cosgrove family that had been connected with the old Robin Hood Hotel in Richmond Hill. The Cosgroves provided bed and board for the MSR line's construction workers for fifty cents a day.

A steam-plant powerhouse to operate the first stretch of the northern line was in Hogg's Hollow at York Mills. As the line progressed past Oak Ridges a second, similar powerhouse was set up at Bond Lake to provide the energy for the extension to Newmarket, where the line arrived in 1899. By 1990 there were five trips a day to Newmarket, but to reach there the track left its Yonge Street route and ran east.

Electric cars were running to Jackson's Point at Lake Simcoe in 1906 and in 1909 they reached their farthest terminus at Sutton, the former Bourchier's Mills. This was a remarkable achievement in the hundred-odd years since Lieutenant-Governor Simcoe made his journey by foot from Holland Landing to Muddy York. His inspiration had been the old Roman colonizers who built the military roads across the moors and bogs of Britain. The inspiration for the electric street-car line had come from American know-how, a source that would have soured Johnny Simcoe, who had a deep antipathy to the republican nation to the south.

The result of this progress? More grumbles, of course. People objected to paying to change cars at the track break. Lengthy delays were caused by the single tracks, when cars put into the lay-bys that were spaced at intervals along the line to allow north and south bound passing. Two elderly ladies, nostalgically recalling 'Old Eglinton' for *The Globe*, described "...the mail coaches which came dashing down Yonge Street from Lake Simcoe and through from Penetang, the driver in the 'boot,' the interior crowded with passengers and the rack behind with trunks and bundles." Then they lamented that "...the advent of the electric cars was hailed by everyone with joy, except the ladies of the community, who could not commission the motorman to bring back parcels as they were in the habit of doing with the 'bus driver'."[69]

There were also complaints that the Metro cars passed by people, went too fast on the downgrade, killed cattle, poultry and dogs and, scandalous to report, the conductors had been seen reading a newspaper.[70] Unwary pedestrians were occasional victims of the unswerving streetcar, but as Doctor Johnson boomed in his dogmatic fashion, the prospect of being run down, like that of being hanged, concentrates the mind wonderfully.

In Toronto the Good, however, minds were wonderfully concentrated by what was little more than a teapot tempest, should the streetcars be run on Sundays? The labour unions at first regarded the proposals to run Sunday streetcars as a cunning move to deprive the worker of his day of rest and to lead eventually to a round-the-clock, seven-days-a-week operation. Then they changed to the opposite tack and supported Sunday cars because they had formed the opinion that the traditional Sabbath restrictions were designed to keep the working man down, docile and obedient.

Other supporters of a Sunday schedule said that it would give the workers their only chance to escape to the fresh air of the countryside. Nonsense, said the opponents, people would wander away from picnics to the local hotels and drunken brawls would be the only outcome from these nature rambles, to say nothing of skylarking in the bushes. Solid citizens and the clergy feared risking "Toronto's future morality for a present few hours of recreation on the Lord's Day."[71]

The dispute provided the public with some harmless diversion for a few years at least. Enthusiasm for fresh air and such healthy habits as an addiction to milk brought a partial lifting of the ban on Sunday cars in 1895 when they were allowed to run for milk deliveries only. It was not until May, 1897, however, that streetcars ran a regular passenger service on Yonge Street on Sundays for the first time in the history of Toronto the Good. Picnic-land had become just a streetcar ride distant.

The *Toronto World*, normally not one of the brighter stars in the newspaper heavens, anticipated in January, 1897 that "What to thousands of Toronto has been an unexplored territory will no doubt be opened up. ...one cannot help thinking that with electric cars running, Richmond Hill will assume more the character of a suburb of Toronto than an outlying country village."

The *World* had a happy knack of sliding over facts. North of Eglinton the villages were not so much suburbia as recreation outlets for the citizens of Toronto. The Northern Railway Company used to have picnics for its employees near the station at Aurora that was also handy to the hotel if rain stopped play, or if the heat made them thirsty. As early as the 1860s there were accounts of these picnics being spoiled by rain and by some of the employees wandering off to hotels

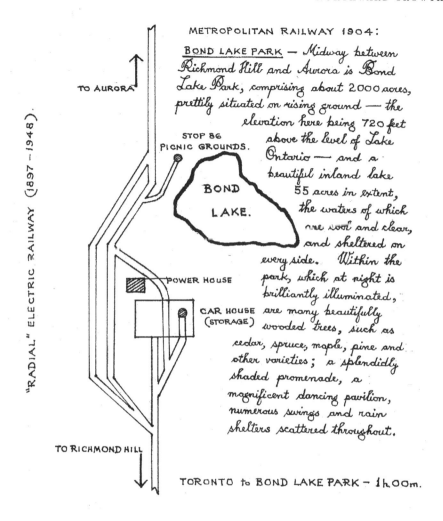

"RADIAL" ELECTRIC RAILWAY (1897 – 1948).

METROPOLITAN RAILWAY 1904:

BOND LAKE PARK — Midway between Richmond Hill and Aurora is Bond Lake Park, comprising about 2000 acres, prettily situated on rising ground — the elevation here being 720 feet above the level of Lake Ontario — and a beautiful inland lake 55 acres in extent, the waters of which are cool and clear, and sheltered on every side. Within the park, which at night is brilliantly illuminated, are many beautifully wooded trees, such as cedar, spruce, maple, pine and other varieties; a splendidly shaded promenade, a magnificent dancing pavilion, numerous swings and rain shelters scattered throughout.

TO AURORA

STOP 86
PICNIC GROUNDS.

BOND LAKE.

POWER HOUSE

CAR HOUSE (STORAGE)

TO RICHMOND HILL

TORONTO to BOND LAKE PARK — 1h.00m.

and becoming drunk and quarrelsome.[72] Another favourite picnic spot was Sutton after the arrival of the electric streetcar line and stories were told of the old radial cars being so overloaded that the passengers had to get out and help to shove them up the hills.

The great place for parties, however, was the old Bond Lake Tavern that had been in business since 1835 at Bond Lake just south of Oak Ridges. It had more than twenty rooms and a spacious ballroom in the building's south end was the popular resort of sleigh-driving parties from Yorkville, Thornhill, Richmond Hill and Newmarket. Curlers from Newmarket and Toronto held matches on the ice-

End of a day's outing ~ Bond Lake, east of Yonge Street.

bound Bond Lake across Yonge Street from the hotel. "The Young People's Societies of Newmarket, Aurora, Kettleby and Richmond Hill, intend holding a grand
picnic at Bond's Lake on Friday, 24th inst." [June, 1892].[73]

So popular did Bond Lake become that early in the 1900s the Metropolitan
Railway Company made a park area and playground there for the benefit of its
employees. The Bond Lake farm had been sold to Mackenzie's outfit by a Mrs.
Bell in 1898 and at the start of the following year the owner of the Tavern, William Legge, sold it to the Company.

Bond Lake was an ideal spot for picnics, bathing and canoeing. At one time a
small paddle-steamer used to churn around the lake for short cruises. It was appropriately named 'The Lady of the Lake,' christened about the middle of the
century by a Miss Mary Steele of Oak Ridges. The streetcars had a stop at a convenient platform by the lake, directly across from the Tavern if one didn't like
boating, or suffered a sudden 'mal-de-mer.'

Fire destroyed the Bond Lake Tavern in September, 1900, and with its destruc-
tion went the last of the old-time Yonge Street inns between Toronto and Newmarket.

The streetcars at first brought visitors and pleasure-seekers, not residents. The population of Richmond Hill, nine hundred in 1884, hung around the one thousand mark up to the First World War. In Thornhill the population stayed near seven hundred from 1870 to the end of the century, after which it very gradually developed as a commuter point for Toronto. At Holland Landing, six hundred was the approximate number of inhabitants during this period. In general, north of Eglinton society was more settled, rural and conservative in comparison with the opportunity-grabbing, the huff-and-puff of Toronto.

Beyond Toronto, beyond the old Muddy York, in spite of so much progress, the road was a remarkably muddy Yonge Street and an irritation to all who had to use it. With the coming of the railways the upkeep of the road had fallen off in the half century following 1850 and there was a universal reluctance to accept the financial responsibility for improvements. Eventually an order-in-council in April, 1865 transferred the York roads from the government to York county at a cost of $72,500 for the dubious privilege of collecting the tolls.

In places like Newmarket that was served directly by the Northern Rail Road, there was a tendency to be complacent about the condition of Yonge Street. With the cheerful optimism of the unaffected the *Newmarket Era* of December 23, 1870 reported that "with the exception of the Toll House south of Holland Landing and North of Richmond Hill; and the completion of the culvert at the Landing, Yonge Street is in thorough repair."

Richmond Hill was less easily satisfied although plank sidewalks and four crosswalks were provided in the village in 1876. They merely became another item in the perennial lamentation on the state of the York roads. The *York Herald* of April 10, 1879 directed "the attention of our village [Richmond Hill] Guardians to the bad state in which our Yonge street crossings are in (sic). With good sidewalks we think good crossings are an absolute necessity, especially for the ladies, on whose behalf we are always ready to speak."

Shades of Sir Walter Raleigh and his cloak-dropping antics in the mud of Merrie England; but clumsy expressions of gallantry fooled nobody. The public, of whatever sex, wanted results for its money, or at least a guarantee that something was being done. In response to the clamour about the state of the road, a committee appointed by the York County Council arrived in cabs at the Palmer House in Richmond Hill to examine the condition of Yonge Street, about which "so much complaint has been made lately."[74] That was in November, 1879. And if the members arrived by cab then the road could not have been quite as bad as its description.

The problem was that nobody liked to pay for the roads and everybody expected a maximum benefit from whatever tolls could be gathered. The upkeep of the road by tolls was a continuous headache. A notice in *The Mail* of April 30, 1875 announcing another tender for the lease of the tolls on the York Roads seems to have had about as much success as it would being published in the kingdom of the blind.

Enthusiasm for the toll system varied in relation to a community's distance from Yonge Street. The *York Herald* of January 12, 1888 reported a meeting at Newmarket where there were strong objections to the continuance of the toll-gate.—"Toll-Gates—At a largely attended meeting held in Newmarket on the 30th ult., the following resolution was carried:—'That our representatives be instructed to move for the abolition of toll-gates and the York Roads to be maintained by the Municipality through or along which they pass. If they find it impossible to carry this scheme that they give their influence to let the roads remain as they are'."

Closer to Yonge Street, in places like Richmond Hill, there was not so much objection to the tollgates as a fear that if the municipalities took over the upkeep of roads from the county these would rapidly deteriorate into trails of mire and misery.—"There is every reason to think that if Yonge Street and the other York roads are left to be maintained by the municipalities through which they pass, they will cease to be good roads, and this will be a detriment to the whole country."[75] In the excitement of dispute this admission that the roads were actually 'good' seems to have passed unnoticed.

The demands for the abolition of the tollgates reached a stalemate in the mid-'nineties. *The Liberal* of October 31, 1895 noted this deadlock between the municipalities that could not agree upon how the expenses for the roads should be shared if they accepted the responsibility for maintenance. Consequently, said the paper, any initiative to abolish the tollgates would have to come from the provincial government. Ontario's Liberal government, however, was hesitant about pushing the issue because many of the farmers on Yonge Street were Grit, or Reform supporters. Any hasty move that might saddle the municipalities with unpopular road costs could endanger the vote.

And so the argument dragged on through 1896, undecided whether the country or the municipalities should charge the toll on the York roads.[76] Finally it was settled that the municipalities should bear the costs for the roads and that the money should be raised by some method other than tolls, but that method could not be agreed upon. The *Aurora Banner* of February 5, 1897 reported a meeting of the Markham and Vaughan Township Councils in the Dominion Hotel, Richmond Hill to discuss the appropriations that each should make for the upkeep of Yonge Street. They could not agree on the best way to make the levy and "the matter was laid over for further consideration."

The dust settled, the decisions were made, and the *Aurora Banner* in February, 1898 closed the play with a brief notice of the sale to a Milton Wells of the toll house one mile south of Aurora.—"After paying the expenses of the two sales [of toll houses] the three municipalities, King, Whitchurch and Aurora, to which the toll houses were handed over by the county, will each realize $17.04."

While the townships were playing this game of 'beggar-my-neighbour' with all the sharpness of a Dickensian contest between Silas Marner and Ebenezer Scrooge, *The Liberal* with a perfectly unconscious irony reprinted an article on the 'Care of Macadam Roads' from the Road Improvement Association of London, England.[77] And that sort of road, as any Englishman would have pointed out, was "deuced expensive, sir." Who would pay the piper? The farmers wanted two levels of assessment. The roads suffered from their heavy, iron-rimmed wagon wheels in the summer, but were scarcely affected by their sleighs and cutters in winter. And they argued that this difference should be reflected in the costs for upkeep.

Squeaking wheels, public opinion and pressure groups eventually have results and in 1894 a Good Roads Association was formed to improve the condition of highways in the province. Out of this developed the Department of Highways, formed in 1900. A decade later, however, and the disgruntlement was still there, evident in the complaints of *The Globe*:

> GOOD ROADS A REAL NEED
> If good roads are the first sign of civilization, the district around Toronto must be 'darkest Canada.' There are portions of Yonge Street and the Lake Shore road that would disgrace a Uganda swamp. For years public-spirited men in the city and in the country have been carrying on a campaign for road-building, and heretofore their efforts have been productive of little improvement. The roads are still quagmires in the spring and fall, and only bold people with urgent business care to use them.

A joint committee representing the City Council, the county
authorities, and those interested in good roads has formulated a
plan of improvement involving the expenditure of $100,000 by the
Provincial Government, $100,000 by the county of York, and
$100,000 by the city of Toronto on the improvement of fifty miles
of the main structure of traffic, such as the Danforth road, Yonge
street, Dundas street, and the Lake Shore road. The approval of
the City Council and of the citizens is necessary to the spending of
this money. It should be granted promptly and unreservedly. The
habit of country life is taking a firm grip on the citizens. Toronto is
becoming too big for the petty policy that would force people to
live within the city limits by leaving the roads unfit for travel and
cutting off car lines at the city boundary. With good roads and fast
Radial cars Toronto's citizens within the next quarter century will
dot the entire region from Oakville on the west to Whitby on the
east with their country homes. And they will be none the less good
citizens because they raise their own fruit and vegetables and keep
their own cows.[78]

The Globe as usual, tended to overblow things. It was, however, thinking big in
the American fashion and even if at times the pushy exuberance for progress
seemed crass, it was a way to achieve goals, and to achieve them quickly.

The vision was still of a city that would mainly expand to east and west, although the picture of urban artisans commuting from country homes with a cow
in every garage and cabbages on every lawn was a touch unrealistic. 'Back to the
land' movements of city residents have never been anything but a source of
amusement and amazement to farmers. Urban life and farming have never mixed,
as was evident in the demarcation between the city and the communities that lay
to the north of its limits. The growing city seemed to suck up and swallow new
portions of east and west in hungry gulps, but the northern parts it bit off in
chunks to be chewed slowly before the next bite.

After Deer Park the next bite took in a portion reaching almost to York Mills.
Immediately north of Deer Park was the little village of Mount Pleasant, of
which the greater part provided a picturesque burial ground for the city of Toronto. The Mount Pleasant cemetery, with a one-and-a-quarter mile frontage on

Yonge Street, was officially opened in November, 1876, and presented an attractive, carefully landscaped vista for passers-by.

It was a vast improvement upon the usual weed tangled plot of oddly leaning stone slabs. Nevertheless, the brochure advertising the Mount Pleasant cemetery overdid the stodgy sentiment enough to make the rough-and-tumble of Valhalla seem a welcome alternative: "Beneath the verdant and flowery sod—beneath the green and waving foliage—amid tranquil shades—where nature weeps in all her dews, and sighs in every bough—and each warbling bird and glittering cascade chants a solemn requiem, the dying generations of this metropolis will henceforth be largely sepulchered."[79] And, need it be said, O'Halloran's Deer Park Hotel would do a large trade as the mourners drank to the memory of the dear departed.

And to talk of graves, there was a tale told about a sleigh with three people arriving late one winter's evening in the yard at O'Halloran's. Two of the occupants got out and headed for the bar for a quick bracer before continuing south to the city. An ostler from the hotel happened at that moment to come out from the stables, and seeing the third occupant not moving asked him why he didn't care to join his two companions at the bar. The reason was very quickly obvious—the man was dead.

The ostler took the shock easily enough and kept his head, because when the two returned from the bar, sufficiently stiffened for the rest of their journey, the 'corpse' inquired if they had enjoyed themselves. At that, the pair fled into the night leaving the sleigh behind with the chuckling ostler. The men were obviously grave-robbers who had hopes of selling their stolen corpse to the medical faculty of the University.

Although nothing was ever decided, Mount Pleasant cemetery may well have been the scene of their crime. To prevent such crimes the cemetery had an octagonal 'dead house' where bodies could be stored during the winter when the frozen ground made grave-digging difficult if not impossible. These 'dead houses' were found only in Ontario and most of them were on Yonge Street. Such houses were provided in the 'sixties and 'seventies at Richmond Hill, Aurora and Newmarket.

Someone who signed himself 'Traveller' wrote a letter dated December 21, 1863 to the *Newmarket Era* advocating 'dead houses': "'The fact that numerous bodies are annually purloined from country churchyards adds much to the importance and necessity for such a building, and all parties who are so unfortunate as to lose any of their relatives will find in this Vault a safe place of deposit until the ensuing spring."

Once past Mount Pleasant, solemn, slow-swaying pine trees frowned over the second-growth trees on the suburban edges and kept fresh the memory of the not-so-distant pioneering days. Here began the hinterland vital to the survival of any city, the start of the true farming country where land husbandry was more important than landscaping. Northward from here on Yonge Street, people generally were still as strong in support of the Grits as their grandfathers had been for William Lyon Mackenzie. "The electors of North York come of sturdy stock. The fathers of the present generation marched down Yonge street with Lyon Mackenzie in the fight for responsible government. The new Family Compact is as distasteful to the electors of today as was that of '37 to their forefathers."[80]

The villages of Davisville and Eglinton had a store of local legends about Mackenzie's 'Last Stand' in the woods below what is now Eglinton Avenue. Although the smoke had long since cleared and the battle's echoes faded among the trees, many bitter memories lingered. The physical reminders for several years afterwards were the battered gateposts of a building that had been struck by a cannon shot from the force that marched against Mackenzie. At a subsequent stage the building was said to have been used as a schoolhouse.

Davisville and Eglinton were joined together in the incorporated village of North Toronto in November, 1889. In April of the following year, North Toronto became an incorporated town, the last step before being taken over by the city.

Davisville was a tiny village with a population around one hundred in 1870 and with a reputation for the manufacture of pottery. The pottery works was started in 1815 by John Davis from whom the village took its name. In 1870 the John Davis who was then running the pottery became the village's first postmaster, the post office being in the grocery store on the northwest corner of what are now Yonge and Imperial Streets.

Davis was a staunch Methodist and gave a quarter of an acre of land just north of the post office to be used for a church site. The father of the Rt. Hon. Lester B. Pearson was at the turn of the century the minister of the Davisville Methodist church, after which the family moved north to Aurora. One of the young Pearson's first memories included somewhat "uncertainly a pottery across the road from our house in Davisville."[81] It might be of interest that the first of the Pearsons to arrive in Canada, the late prime minister's great-grandfather Marmaduke, bought John Macdonald's dry goods store and property, the 'Large 103' on Yonge Street.

The Pearsons were originally from Dublin and so must have felt at ease in

North Toronto with its Protestant Irish heritage, Methodist-disciplined society, and Orange Lodge domination. Yonge Street in the 'nineties was often the scene of the Orangemen's 'Glorious Twelfth' of July parades led by pipe bands and a fancy-dress version of King Billy on his white horse, encouraged by raucous anti Catholic songs like 'The Sash My Father Wore ' Drink and the Devil, the elect decided, would take care of their opponents.

Hotels, however, were still good business, even if drink was frowned upon. There were several in North Toronto. Lemon's Davisville Hotel was on the southeast corner of Yonge Street and Davisville Avenue and Eglinton had more than a fair share for its size. These places were hard hit when 'local option' was passed for North Toronto in 1908 and the township voted for temperance.

Eglinton was the larger of the two villages that made up North Toronto. Toward the end of the century it was a straggling village of some seven hundred inhabitants and its way of life was of a piece with Davisville and the other small villages along Yonge Street. Eglinton remained a relatively small farming community until the 1890s, when the expanding city brought it almost literally out of the woods.

The sole religious centre of the neighbourhood was, for many years, the old Methodist church on the southeast corner of what are today Yonge Street and Glengrove Avenue. The half-acre of land for this church had been given by Jesse Ketchum in 1830 and a small brick building was erected on it by the Wesleyan Methodists in 1834. Nearby stood an old log schoolhouse where a Mr. Moulton was the master in the 'fifties and 'sixties. Life in Eglinton did not change much, and even by the end of the First World War, Eglinton Avenue was little more than a trail that crossed Yonge Street, marked by Coon's Feed Store on the northwest corner. The store later became the Eglinton Restaurant.

Two elderly ladies recalled the early days in Eglinton for *The Globe* in 1910. The life that they described was a simple, self-contained affair in which people made their own amusements. While Toronto griped about winter's slippery sidewalks and the streetcars piling snow, winter hid the rough roads in North Toronto and made sleighing parties a great favourite with the young people.

Each generation eventually takes refuge in its own particular nostalgia, however, and one of Moulton's old pupils, nearing seventy in 1910, said to the old ladies that the 'old way' in education was much better, there being 'much more spontaneity and free-will' in Moulton's day. Spontaneity, perhaps—but it was very much hit-and-miss, with the quality of the education depending upon the qualifications of the individual master. One-room schoolhouses were better known for producing nostalgia than for producing well-rounded scholars.

It is nostalgia and legend that nonetheless warm the cold facts of history and give life to memory, although not everyone would welcome a return of the often less than good old days. The old ladies "used to have a woman come and wash a whole day for a quarter, and a seamstress would also do a day's sewing for a quarter." And, so they said, "of all the old [market] gardeners around Toronto very few that lived on or rented places ever made enough to keep them in their old age."[82]

Life in Eglinton stayed close to the edge of necessity, unlike Toronto's entrepreneurial flights and speculations. Adaptability, rather than innovation, was the way of the world north of Eglinton and old-established ways were not much brought to question. "In old Eglinton it seems, marriage, though acknowledged as indispensable, was looked upon by the contracting parties as a dangerous secret not to be allowed to leak out, even when the event itself was to take place. Consequently, the bride would wend her way to the church in one sheltered direction, the groom in another equally guarded manner. The penalty of letting the cat out of the bag was the charivari, conducted in all its early gusto. Church weddings were almost unheard of, however, and most happy pairs were united in the best rooms of the bride's parents."[83]

The charivaris were probably the noisiest events to rattle Eglinton since that December afternoon in 1837 when the day's crystal-brittle stillness had been shattered by the cannon-shots to quell Mackenzie at Montgomery's Tavern.

Montgomery himself was sentenced to life imprisonment for his part in Mackenzie's Rebellion, but escaped to the United States from confinement at Kingston and was eventually pardoned along with the other exiles in 1843.[84] He returned to his old haunt on Yonge Street and built a two-storey hotel a very short distance south of his tavern that had been burned in the immediate aftermath of the skirmish on December 7, 1837. The destroyed tavern had stood near the southwest corner of the present Montgomery Avenue and Yonge Street.

As business prospered, Montgomery moved to the heart of the city in 1855 and started the Franklin House at 141 Yonge Street, two or three doors north of Queen. Three years later he sold his rebuilt hotel to Charles McBride of Willowdale, who renamed the place Prospect House, whether from the view or an anticipated financial success is anybody's guess.

McBride certainly did well for himself. He had a farm off Yonge Street just south of the present Fairlawn Avenue that he is credited with having opened up.

Sometime in the early 'seventies he bought the old Finch's Tavern on Yonge Street, at the modern Finch Avenue where John Finch had leased Montgomery's former 'Sickle and Sheaf.' Finch's was then torn down and its timbers used to build McBride's Bedford Park Hotel on his farm south of Fairlawn, where the hotel stood until well into the present century.

Prospect House had a much briefer existence, being destroyed by fire in November, 1881. The same fire ripped through the Masonic Hall, built in 1874 across the road from the hotel. Grander buildings soon took their place and kept the Yonge Street-Montgomery Avenue corner as the centrepiece of Eglinton. The Orange Lodge was nearby.

After the fire the vacant site of the Prospect House was bought by John Oulcott who in 1883 built there the large, three-storey, brick Eglinton House. It was well-provided with driving sheds and stables for its country clients, becoming a lively centre for horse auctions in the district and for the celebration of deals, although it was turned into a temperance hotel with the local option of 1908. Oulcott owned the hotel from 1883 to 1912, with a variety of proprietors among whom, in 1891, were Brunskill and Munshaw, partners from two well-known old families in the Thornhill-Richmond Hill area.

In the 1920s the Eglinton House was being used as the North Toronto post office and in the following decade it was demolished. The lot where the Masonic Hall had stood was purchased by the village and the Eglinton town hall was built there in 1882, becoming the town hall for North Toronto after amalgamation with Davisville. It was knocked down in 1931 to make way for a police station.

The Reverend Henry Scadding said that the name Eglinton somehow came from the mock mediaeval Eglinton Tournament held by the 13th Earl of Eglinton on his Ayrshire estate in 1839. Another story claims, however, that Montgomery the tavern owner chose the name in memory of "an estate in Scotland whence he came."[85] Scadding's story seems a shade far-fetched. It should be remembered that he was what the Scots would call a bit of a blether, with a fondness for titled society and the British connection, and no liking for Reformers of Montgomery's stamp. He was not likely to admit that there was any link between the village's name and its tavern-keeper.

The version connecting Eglinton with Montgomery would seem to be on firmer ground. Although Montgomery was born in New Brunswick where his Loyalist family had moved from the States, he may well have fancied the name Eglinton because it happened that the family name of the Earls of Eglinton was

Montgomerie. Only a definite date for the first use of Eglinton for the village might establish the truth.

Local legend also provided the story that the land on which Montgomery built his tavern of Rebellion notoriety was given to him by James Harvey Price, a Welshman who was a highly successful lawyer in York. The reason for this gift was that Montgomery was at one time supposed to have been Price's coachman. Stories of the Montgomery family naturally make no mention of this, but the fact remains that the tavern was built on land which formed part of the Price estate.

Price made the mistake of backing the Reform cause of W.L. Mackenzie. He advanced money to Mackenzie, but with the failure of the Rebellion he realized that he was unlikely ever to see the money again. Financial difficulties were the reward of his unfortunate political enthusiasm and he was forced to sell part of his estate and the impressive, English-style stone house, Castlefield, that he had built upon it.

One of the more fanciful tales of Mackenzie's escape after his débacle at Montgomery's Tavern features Castlefield as the place where a sympathetic housekeeper hid the carroty-wigged fugitive in a large cradle in the kitchen. Beyond the febrile imagination of the housekeeper there is nothing to verify the incident.

In 1842 Castlefield and one hundred and twenty-five acres of land running from Yonge Street to Bathurst were sold to Franklin Jackes for nine hundred and eighty-five Spanish dollars, a preferred currency of the time. Price eventually went back to England, a sadder and wiser man, having lost much of his fortune through backing an ineptly-organized political enthusiasm and having learned that betting on politics is as risky as horse-racing but less fun. The Mackenzies get the star billing and the Prices pay the bills. Franklin Jackes, on the other hand, had been as lucky as Price had been unlucky in taking a gamble. He took a chance on the then very uncertain business of sending goods by sea and scooped a windfall on five pounds that he used to buy a pessimistic shipping agent's interest in two ships long overdue in Toronto and believed to be sunk.

Gambling on the uncertain trade of the day and dealing in real estate were the great Canadian lottery games of the nineteenth century. And the games could be rough. Jackes may have been home free when he took his chance on a flour shipment, but when Benjamin Thorne, the miller who christened Thornhill, was ruined by the total loss of one of his transatlantic shipments, he took a solitary walk in the meadow behind his home and shot himself. It was win some, lose some, with God being as often thanked as Dame Luck for the windfalls of good fortune.

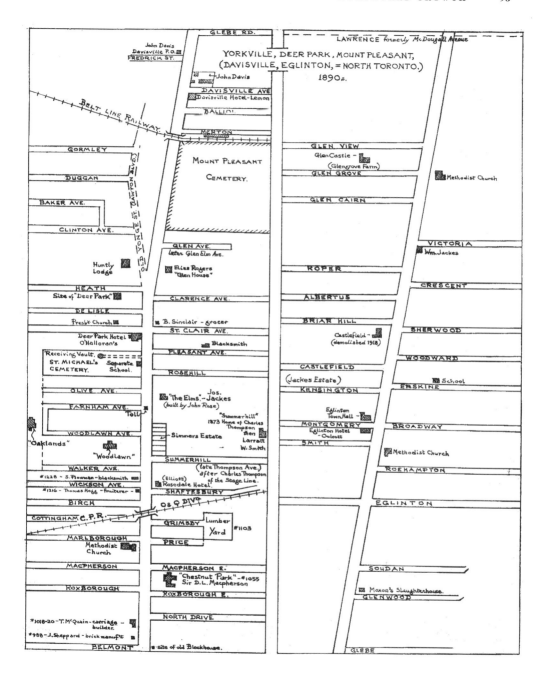

YORKVILLE, DEER PARK, MOUNT PLEASANT,
(DAVISVILLE, EGLINTON, = NORTH TORONTO.)
1890s.

Jackes had a bakery business on King Street across from the present St. Law-rence Market, but with his sudden, happy profit he gave up the business and re-tired to the country in 1835. His first country residence before moving to Castlefield was a large frame structure called the Yellow House that stood on the west side of Yonge Street just below what is now Glengrove Avenue. After the Yellow House, Castlefield was the home of the Jackes family until 1885, when the property was sold. The house was demolished in 1918.

The estates of Price and Jackes were in an area favoured by other aspirants to the style of country gentlemen, whose homes have left their names upon the lo-cal maps. Shrewd real estate and business deals generated the money for this new gentry to set up country homes where formerly had been the bailiwick of pioneer, farmer, tanner, miller and tavern-keeper.

The area of Glengrove, where the Yellow House had once stood, was the farm that James Beaty, successful leather merchant, toll-road lessee and MPP, bought for his summer home, Glen Grove, in 1855. Glengrove Avenue was at one time the driveway to the mansion, grandly known as Glen Castle, that stood on the property. There seems to have been some confusion whether Glen Castle was one and the same with Ansley Castle, located on what is now Glengrove Avenue and

Ansley Castle — built by Alfred Ansley
(of Christie Flats) in 1909, later sold
to J. P. Bickle.

Heather Street. The Ansleys, however, did not build their castle there until 1909 and it was demolished in 1925. On the south side of what became Glengrove Avenue a character by the name of King Dodds started a race-track in 1887, but it folded after two years of operation.

Apart from some all-too-brief moments in summer and fall, there was often a sullen harshness in the air about these stately homes, grim-shadowed like the Scotland of Shakespeare's *Macbeth*. It was too forbidding an atmosphere to support grandiose living such as a feudal squire with ample means and a tenant host at his command might enjoy. That style Canada could not provide. The countryside's dreary, wet-black silhouettes against muddy-grey or snow-white landscapes had all the bleakness of a Russian novel.

Attempts to recreate the pattern of England with social magnificence and the like of the Eglinton Hunt Club were more in defiance of Nature than in harmony with her. England could not be grafted on to the Yonge Street countryside that had no place for the softness of Swinburne's "deep wet ways by grey old gardens.'

If anything, the atmosphere about Toronto encouraged flamboyance rather than grandeur, resulting in the occasional aberration like Sir Henry Pellatt's Casa Loma. Affectations and associations came to mean more than reality. There was no real imperial sentiment left, such as that which had inspired Simcoe to create his Yonge Street as a link for strategic points. What remained was an attachment to an imperial dream, to the glory and brilliance reflected from the high noon of Britain's imperial grandeur.

As part of this attachment, Toronto's 'old guard' held close to the military association, drumming up support for the militia and involvement in Britain's wars, while cursing the French for putting up the practical argument from the Canadian viewpoint that such involvement was unnecessary. For a select Anglophile handful there was an irresistible magnetism in the pageant of England's glory and the heroic traditions and legends from the colourful, adventurous skirmishes on the edges of her empire, in Zululand, the Khyber hills and the African veldt.

A few took an active part. Colonel A.R. Dunn won his Victoria Cross in the charge of the Light Brigade in the Crimea and later died from a hunting accident while serving in the campaign against Emperor Theodore of Abyssinia during 1867-8. The *York Herald* noted briefly on September 4, 1879 that "Mr. Clarke Gamble's son has died in Afghanistan," during the Second Afghan War, 1878-80.

There were some highlights of military enthusiasm during the Fenian Raids of 1866 and 1870; in the Sudan campaign of 1884-5 when French Canadian voyageurs hauled General Wolseley's boats past the cataracts of the Nile; in the Northwest Rebellion of 1885; and, of course, the Boer War. In general, however, the military experience was vicarious.

In 1910 *The Globe* was proudly reporting the activities of the Queen's Own Rifles of Canada which Colonel Sir Henry Pellatt had taken overseas to England to participate in the late summer manoeuvres being held there. Bands, cheering crowds, the Kiplingesque camaraderie of warriors and Sir Henry in company with knighted, decorated veterans of many campaigns—all shed a romantic light over the grim art of war whose reality the poet of Canada's Yukon, Robert Service, had tried to reveal in *The March of the Dead*:

> They left us on the veldt-side, but we felt we couldn't stop
> On this our England's crowning festal day;
> We're the men of Magersfontein, we're the men of Spion Kop,
> Colenso,—we're the men who had to pay.
> We're the men who paid the blood-price. Shall the grave be
>   all our gain?
> You owe us. Long and heavy is the score.

Toronto ignored it. *The Globe* preferred photographs of the Queen's Own, alive and fit, marching down Yonge Street. In 1910 the greatest hazards were the unsanitary conditions in England. During Colonel Pellatt's triumphant visit, one of Canada's casualties was Sir Casimir Gzowski's son, Lieutenant R.M. Gzowski, a victim of typhoid and pneumonia.

For many Englishmen themselves, the early adventure of Canada was fading. Arctic exploration, trading and soldiering had lost much of their appeal. It was not to be the land for younger sons, for empire-builders, nor for the types that were reported wandering into southern Africa with Cecil Rhode's pioneer column—soldiers, sailors, cadets of good family and no special occupation, cricketers, three parsons and a Jesuit.

It would, nevertheless, seem from all accounts that Canada had her fair share of remittance men, the ne'er-do-wells of an imperial order that was described as being 'a vast system of outdoor relief for Britain's upper classes.' That, at least, is how James S. Mill described it. The industrious Scots and unforgiving Irish of Upper Canada had no time for these hangers-on and neither did many of those people whose pioneering farmer forebears had come up from Pennsylvania and New York.

The Globe, Oct. 8, 1910:
"Queen's Own Rifles Welcomed in Quebec and Toronto."
Marching Down Yonge Street.

The serious-minded imperial Englishman preferred the opportunity to rule and administer, to judge and police his empire's charges with a benevolent paternalism. For him, pioneering was tedious, farming hard and business dull. If he thought of Canada at all, it was the Hudson's Bay Company or the Royal North West Mounted Police that usually came to mind.

Canadians, particularly those settled in the little villages on Yonge Street north of the city, were an independent lot, drawing heavily on the tradition of 'freemen of the soil' that several of their ancestors had brought with them from the States. Sometimes slow to arouse, they could become obstreperous when they felt that they were being pushed around by a faceless officialdom.

An interesting example of this was in Toronto when the Toronto Railway Company first introduced the 'Pay-as-you-enter' scheme for its streetcars. *The Globe* of December 8, 1910 headlined the story of the dispute that resulted:

MOB SMASHES STREET CARS, PARALYSES WHOLE SYSTEM
Pay-as-you-enter System is condemned by Sufferers.

Windows had been smashed in some of the Yonge Street cars and Mayor Geary called a public meeting in Massey Hall, where the 'high-handed methods' of the Toronto Railway Company in respect to its 'Pay-as-you-enter' regulations were roundly condemned. On the following day *The Globe* urged a Canadian spirit of moderation in spite of the provocation to the public. "The mob that smashed the windows of the street cars was, like all mobs, composed of a crowd of young fools, with here and there a more seasoned blackguard, in whom for a time the beast had gained the upper hand."

In North Toronto, too, in October of the same year, there was a dispute with the Metropolitan Railway, that was by then the York Radial Railway, over the service on Yonge Street. The company wanted to run double tracks through the township. In return the town councillors wanted concessions on fares and mileage from the north limit of the town to the North Toronto crossing, during working hours, ten tickets for a quarter, or fifty for a dollar.[86] The proposals were withdrawn, however, and the deal fell through.

1910 was a bad year for the streetcar companies. Mackenzie's Toronto Street Railway employees had threatened to strike in August in a disagreement over wages and hours of labour. At one point the men demanded that the company supply stools for the conductors in its cars. *The Globe* recommended voluntary arbitration and more or less suggested that both parties in the dispute grow up and stop squabbling like spoiled kids. "It is not out of place to remind the disputants once more that the people of Toronto, who are the owners of the franchise of the streets, and who must have the transit service maintained continuously, will not tamely submit to have it indefinitely interrupted simply because two parties to a dispute will not come to terms."[87]

William Mackenzie then issued an ultimatum and offered the men an increase of one cent per hour on their current pay scale. With the aid of some further arbitration the strike was averted.

Neither did the company receive any pats on the back for a civic conscience when the public heard of the amount of the fine for disobeying the Toronto Railway's new bylaw of December 1, 1910 "prohibiting spitting, smoking, or the carrying of lighted cigars, cigarettes or pipes on the street cars of the city."[88]

"As to the fine, some criticism has been made on account of its severity. The matter of the penalty, however, is prescribed by statute of the Ontario Legislature. A twenty-dollar fine may seem unduly harsh, but it will at least show that the offense is not regarded as a trivial one."[89]

The public lament simply continued, like the wailing of a Greek chorus—the Toronto Railway was trying to run its system 'on the cheap,' and the Christmas Eve edition of *The Globe* wound up the year with a complaint about the rudeness of the motormen and conductors and the question, "Should Toronto expropriate the Street Railway?"

Whatever Toronto may have thought of his operation, it didn't affect Mackenzie's prestige with his peers. He became Sir William in the 1911 New Year's Honours List for his work as president of the Canadian Northern Railway.

Before the middle of January, however, his Toronto Railway Company officials were again lambasted in the press, being indicted on the counts that they neglected "to take reasonable precautions for the protection of the lives, safety, health, property and comfort of the public in not equipping their cars with proper fenders, guards or appliances, lights or signals,—that the traffic on the streets was impeded by the cars, and that the company did not supply a sufficient number of cars to carry those who wanted to ride on them, and that they neglected to take precautions to prevent overcrowding of the cars."[90] And tossed in for the grand slam were objections to the way in which women had to squeeze into packed streetcar aisles, in a way that no decent woman should have to tolerate.

To keep the grumble-pot on the bubble, the issue of a railway viaduct over the Esplanade was brought up for the umpteenth time. "The people are up in arms everywhere against level crossings on account of the large number killed. There are about forty of these crossings, which are very dangerous to life and limb, particularly the one at the foot of Yonge Street."[91]

In the summer of 1910 it had been proposed to raise the railway tracks above the Esplanade with the costs being shared by the city and the railway companies. The Grand Trunk agreed, but the CPR objected by lodging an appeal to stop the proposal and *The Globe* then howled that the big railway companies persistently discriminated against Toronto and favoured Montreal.[92]

It was perhaps, in a spirit of tit-for-tat that a CPR conductor was fined $20 and costs for blocking traffic at the foot of Yonge Street "for longer than the period allowed by the city bylaws."93 A policeman had timed the crossing of the forty-five car freight train—seven minutes.

And if it wasn't enough that trains were cluttering the streets, the papers ech-

oed the annoyance of the respectable section of Toronto's public that took a dim
view of the number of drunks to be seen on Yonge Street during business hours.[94]
Women, of course, did not go into bars, but they could get liquor from a licensed
shop; a danger that alarmed *The Globe*, the watchdog of propriety. "The mothers
of Canada must remain sober and self-respecting, and the shop license is a greater
peril to them than the open bar to the men."[95]

If drink was the curse of the working classes in the city, it was a boon to the
inn-keeping business and the distillery-owners beyond the city limits of North
Toronto. The days of the dipper attached to the tin bucket full of whisky for free
in the back of the country store for travel-thirsty customers were fast disappearing, however, and even the number of licenses was being reduced. In the final
years of the nineteenth century the licensed taverns, the distilleries and mills of
whatever description would dwindle to a meagre comparison with their former
number.

At York Mills, exactly where the city's official 'edge' fell away into the driver's
despair that was Hogg's Hollow, had stood the grist and saw mills of James Hogg.
The city had finally expanded to the northern limit of the town of North Toronto. 1911 had begun with 299 to 273 votes in favour of merging the township
with the city, but Toronto's aldermen did not want annexation because they already had enough to look after. It was not until December 15, 1912 that North
Toronto became part of the city.

Where York Mills began, the land still belonged to J. and W. Hogg, heirs of the
redoubtable Hogg the Miller, the Scot who had supported W.L. Mackenzie until
he felt that 'Wee Mac' had gone 'all widdershins' and become too unstable to be
an affective leader. The old mills lasted for many years on the main branch of the
Don River, just south of the present York Mills Road. Hogg's sons started a general store on the property.

The family's old occupation was kept in mind with the name of the Jolly Miller
hotel that stands on what was the Hogg's land on the east side of Yonge Street,
south of the old manse where C.W. Jefferys, the noted artist and illustrator, lived
and worked in the 1920s. Jolly was hardly the word to describe the dour, argu-
mentative James Hogg, but it had a better ring to it than did the sound of York
Mills hotel, as the place had been called when it was the second of that name to
be built on the site about 1860.

Life in general wasn't very jolly, anyway, in the country districts where the streetcars took their summer weekend loads from the city to enjoy the fresh air and picnics. While the city newspapers complained about the roads, the railways, the streetcar service and the drunks, interspersed with the Empire's news, the local papers gave advice to farmers and printed long litanies of accidents, illnesses and deaths affecting their district's residents. There were deaths from lockjaw and drowning, sickness from fevers and infections and injuries from falls and farm implements. The rural life was not always a happy one.

Both city and country newspapers would carry articles, stories and jokes that pointed up the difference between the two ways of life. A good illustration of this was the following somewhat long-winded version of today's 'morning smile' that appeared in the *Aurora Banner* during June, 1898. A newly-married, well-educated young city lady who wanted to lend a hand with the dinner that was being prepared by her country-bred cook:

> "Now, Biddy, what are we to have for dinner?—Chicken would be nice."
> "Why, mum, they're in their feathers yet."
> "Oh, then serve them that way. The Ancient Romans always cooked their peacocks with the feathers on. It will be a surprise for hubby."
> "It will that, mum. ..."

The point of that little tableau wasn't hard to see.

The attitude of the country was like old Hardcastle's in Goldsmith's *She Stoops to Conquer*, when his wife asked him why they did not take an occasional trip into the city "to rub off the rust a little?" Toronto could be easily substituted for London in his reply that such a trip would bring back enough "vanity and affectation to last them a whole year.—I wonder why London cannot keep its own fools at home! In my time, the follies of the town crept slowly among us, but now they travel faster than a stage coach. Its fopperies come down not only as inside passengers, but in the very basket." The streetcar sped up the process even more.

And where the city papers echoed a rather sentimental adulation of Britannia and her belongings, the country press supported her for rather more down-to-earth reasons than those of Auld Lang Syne. The *Aurora Banner* that had resounded to the Liberal Edward Blake's cry of 'Canada First' in October, 1874 was blazing the following Liberal mottoes in February, 1896—"Our town, Our Country and Our Queen," "Success to Our Manufacturers" and "Free Trade England's

Glory." This was less from an admiration for England than from being disgruntled with the Tories' 'National Policy' of a protective tariff, a tariff "founded on no principle but that of grab."[96]

More intriguing than politics were the elopements, domestic disputes and hints of scandals that made the very stuff of local newspaper stories. In April, 1875 Charles Playter of the prominent old Quaker pioneer family accused William Thompson, a farm labourer from Richmond Hill, of having the cheekiness to try to elope with his daughter, Lottie Playter. Democracy had its limits, even in the country.

A more hilarious incident took place in Aurora during the summer of 1899. A character by the name of Blanchard took off from Maple with a Mrs. Baxter, whose husband followed them in a hastily harnessed trap—accompanied by Mrs. Blanchard. This runaway derby ended when the pursuit caught up with its quarry at Yonge and Wellington Streets in Aurora. As the *Aurora Banner* of June 9 described it, "there was a hot time" at the corner where a first-class domestic dust-up took place until the arrival of the local constable, who finally persuaded everybody to go home—with a warning "not to let it happen again."

Then there was the pair of bachelor farmers who took a day's outing in a gig with two young married ladies and the small child of one of the women. Their clandestine trip came to a tragic end when the young spark who was driving the one-horse trap was fired by a Lothario-élan to race the Newmarket train to the railway crossing. The train won. As I remember the story, the horror-fascinated spectators found one survivor of the accident, the small child who had been thrown clear by the collision and was wailing forlornly at the side of the tracks.

At Holland Landing, there was in April, 1898 a family quarrel that took a particularly nasty turn, but its ending will be familiar to all who have been frustrated in attempts at justice by wives who will not testify against their husbands.

The *Aurora Banner* reported that a Mr. Eli Roland, during an argument over an axe that he accused one of his sons of spoiling, took a swipe at his wife with the axe. His son managed to divert the blow from his mother, but was hit on the head in the course of the scuffle, enraging the father even more, so that he took a second swing at the boy. At this point in the hatchet drama one of the daughters joined in to pull the father back from doing any more harm. Old dad then chased everybody out of the house and locked himself in until the neighbours arrived. In court, the son, who had not been badly hurt, said that his injury was an accident, and the others testified that the incident was simply a 'family affair.'

Until as late as the 1920s there stood at Holland Landing a red brick house that was known for having the first tin roof in the district. Located on lot 107 on Yonge Street in East Gwillimbury, it was also famous for having had one of the village's most cantankerous residents under that roof. Its owner in 1850 had been Henry Blackstone, a lawyer and grandson of the great English jurist, Sir William Blackstone who had written the commentaries on the laws of England. Henry's commentaries were inspired by the bottle.

He was given to drinking bouts in which he would hold forth belligerently against whoever would give him an argument. His last argument is commemorated at Holland Landing—by his grave. While he was airing his boozily bellicose views in Robert Playter's tavern at Holland Landing (St. Alban's) on the night of August 22, 1852, some characters who differed with him expressed their disagreement by the primitive but positive expedient of punches that proved fatal for Henry.

Nothing much seems to have been done about those involved, a broth of 'bhoys' called Torrence, Fleming, Flannigan and Dwyer, whose names don't indicate that they would be very sympathetic to Blackstone's Tory English attitudes.[97]

Henry was probably lucky to have lasted as long as he did, if some of the stories about him are to be believed. He was the first lawyer in Newmarket in the 1840s and that Reform-minded place no doubt became so hot for him that it was a choice of removing to Holland Landing or being run out of town on a rail. While in Newmarket he tangled with one of the local Quakers, Martin Bogart of Garbutt Hill and Bogart's Mills. Like most of the Quakers, Martin was a Reform supporter, a political affiliation that was a red rag to true-blue Tory Blackstone who, when in his cups, was very free with his insults.

Seeing Bogart in a tavern one day, Henry announced in his usual ale-bold way that he would use "every damned rebel for a back-log"—and pointed to the open fireplace near the bar. Martin, without any qualms about the Quaker belief that 'peace is the way,' promptly heaved Blackstone into the fireplace alongside the charred log, scattering ashes everywhere. The floor was cleaned with Blackstone serving as the mop and then he was dumped back into the fireplace to the huge delight of the customers. Henry had to borrow some clothes from the tavern-keeper before heading for home more subdued than when he had arrived.[98]

It was the like of such quarrels and problems resulting from drink that encouraged a determined crackdown on the number of liquor-licensed hotels at the end of the century. The countryside was all 'Methodists, Staunch Reformers and Temperance,' although the likes of Blackstone with strong Tory feelings might well bang their jorums on the bar and sing like Tony Lumpkin—

> When Methodist preachers come down,
> A-preaching that drinking is sinful,
> I'll wager the rascals a crown,
> They always preach best with a skinful.

One Newmarket hotel that lost its license in the purge was well known even in Blackstone's time there—the North American Hotel, chopped by the license commissioners in August, 1898. This was not a popular move with either the local farmers or the temperance enthusiasts, the old North American being something of an institution by that time, but the commissioners were adamant that one hotel had to be cut and so its license went. Crusades and sentiment do not always go well together.

A prohibition vote held at this time did result in a very small majority in favour, but not enough to have it enforceable by law. Prohibition, or 'going dry,' had to be decided by local choice. It was probably the best thing that could be done in a situation where feelings ran so high that an acceptable compromise was almost impossible. There were still enough diehards of the school of old Colonel Talbot who had detested 'Methodists, total abstainers and all disloyal persons.'

Earlier in 1882, the Cooks Act was introduced to limit the number of licensed shops, but it had not been very successful. The holders of licenses were to be restricted to the business of selling only liquor, which was a less severe measure than the 1878 Scott Act (Canada Temperance Act) that would prohibit the sale of liquor in shops, but according to the newspapers these acts were violated everywhere. Instead of one saloon properly licensed, every store, "cobbler's stall and all," had whisky for sale.[99]

The moral shindig and the roars of righteousness on the subject of alcohol did not deafen the practical-minded to the ruthless logic of profit-and-loss. The *York Herald* of November 6, 1884, commenting on the area of Richmond Hill, remarked that "Mr. John Palmer is one of the largest taxpayers in the village, his taxes amounting to about one-sixteenth of the whole, besides having to pay for a license to carry on his hotel business. However much conscientious scruples may exist against the business of dealing in intoxicants, it cannot but be admitted that every consideration should be shown to those who are legally qualified, and who respect the Law under which they sell."

And no two ways about it, until the 'local options' at the beginning of the century hit at the drinking class, and it was legion, hotel-keeping could be a remarkably profitable trade.

John Palmer's Palmer House on lot 46 west on Yonge Street had, until 1872, been the old Stage Hotel and it was virtually the hub of the village of Richmond Hill, where it stood on the southwest corner of Yonge and Arnold Streets. A John Kelly was its proprietor for many years:

> THE PALMER HOUSE
> RICHMOND HILL
> This fine hotel is fitted with all the modern
> appliances for health and comfort. Best brands of
> liquors and cigars. Sample rooms for com-
> mercial travellers. 'Busses meet all trains.
> Rates $1.00 per day.
> JOHN KELLY, Proprietor[100]

Regardless of the *York Herald's* plummy phrases about those "who respect the Law under which they sell," when talking of John Palmer, his hotel sometimes passed the Plimsoll mark of legality. In 1896, John Kelly was fined on two charges: one for selling liquor on Sundays, the other for selling drink to a W. Cooper after being told not to do so.[101] Such injunctions were the quickest way of curbing the most outrageous drunks of any locality.

By 1898 Kelly had gone and Walter Hulse was the proprietor, advertising that in addition to the buses meeting the trains, "electric cars pass the door." This improved passenger traffic also encouraged a dentist to travel every Monday from Toronto to Richmond Hill, where he set up his office in the Palmer House. Before the electric streetcar, between the 'seventies and early 'nineties, the dentist's visits had been only once a month—a stagecoach a day had kept the dentist away, until the end of the century.

John Palmer, Jnr., became the hotel's proprietor early in 1900 when Hulse went off to start the Hulse Hotel nearby in Maple. One old resident of Richmond Hill remembers John Palmer as "a fine, well set up fellow—but he was cute—he was forever having lawsuits, but he lost only one of them."[102] He had to be sharp, however, because the hotel business was a highly competitive one in the villages. The successful ones did a roaring business—in some cases almost literally, as patrons got "roarin' fu'..." like Burns's Tam O'Shanter.

TRENCH CARRIAGE WORKS   DOMINION HOUSE HOTEL   PALMER HOUSE HOTEL

Looking south on Yonge Street from Richmond Hill "radial" car stop ~ c.1900.

Two other hotels in Richmond Hill had been granted liquor licenses along with the Palmer House in 1876. These were the Cosgrove's Robin Hood that had been Velie's in 1873 and then Walter Lemon's in 1875, and Pagree's Dominion Hotel, both on lot 46 east side of Yonge Street, across from the Palmer House. In February, 1895 the two-storey, brick Dominion Hotel with its stables and driving shed was put up for sale.[103]

Small though the village was, there had even been a fourth hotel in the 'eighties, the Grand Central whose proprietor was a C. Chamberlin. It took the place of the old White Hart Hotel that had burned down, its site supposedly where Rowland Burr, a well-to-do Quaker mill-owner, built a house in the 1820s.

Milling had been the great occupation throughout much of the nineteenth century in the region that stretched along Yonge Street from York Mills to Thornhill, Richmond Hill and Aurora. Burns may have written lilting lyrics about the "dusty peck brings the dusty siller," but the profits of the milling game were not easily come by and there were hazards enough to belie the notion of its being as jolly as the songs would have it. Fire, dust explosions and floods like the great flood of 1878 that wrought havoc in Thornhill, from which its mills never really recovered were far too common.

Thornhill was perhaps the most thriving of these milling villages, its focal point being Benjamin Thorne's old mill site on lot 32 on the west side of Yonge Street. Sometime after Thorne's suicide in 1847, the Hawthorn Mineral Springs House was built by John Langstaff on this lot. Eventually it became the Thornhill Golf Club house.

With a pioneering versatility, John Langstaff, whose family was among the earliest settlers in Thornhill, ran a steam mill on the northeast corner of what is now Yonge Street and Langstaff Road, across from the Cooks' Yorkshire House in the late 'seventies:

> Patent Eave-trough and Water-
> spout for the Dominion.
>
> At $6 per hundred feet. Also flooring and other
> Lumber dressed, sap buckets, pails, cider mills,
> washing machines, shingles, felloes, sawn and
> bent material for buggies and sleighs.
>   For particulars address
>   JOHN LANGSTAFF
>   Steam Mills, Langstaff, P.O.[104]

Among the earliest mills was the sawmill at the back of lots 37 and 38 on the west side of Yonge Street, belonging to the Dexter family that had an unhappy moment of prominence in 1815 when young John Dexter shot Henry Vandebergh during a quarrel on Yonge Street. Dexter was found guilty of murder and hanged for his unfortunate outburst of uncontrolled temper.

The old Pomona Mills on lot 30 east were operated by John Brunskill from 1840 until his death in 1870. They were destroyed during the three days of torrential rains and floods in September, 1878 that took out bridges and wrecked roads and mills from Thornhill to Hunter's sawmill at York Mills. Like the biblical floods these marked the end of an era. By the 'eighties most of the old mills had disappeared, particularly those that were not converted to steam, as was done with the mill that was built where Hunter's had been. Perhaps the very last of the mills in the area was the steam-driven sawmill set up in Thornhill by a John Wice in 1910 and lasting until 1941.

Another place to profit during the boom in the grain trade and milling business was Aurora. Growing up on the site of an old Indian village, Aurora was first

136 Wellington Street East, Aurora.
"The Railroad" Hotel (Beresford's).
Built c.1856, on east side of the railway
(Ontario, Simcoe & Huron, then the
Northern Railway Co., after 1888)

known to its settlers as Machell's Corners after Richard Machell who ran a general store in the village opposite Charles Doan's house on Yonge Street. Doan, who had been arrested for supporting Mackenzie in 1837, became the first postmaster of Aurora, where he had a large brick general store after his release in the 1840s.

It was Doan who chose the name of Aurora for the village, perhaps believing that the Goddess of the Dawn would be an appropriate symbol to usher in an era of prosperity for the place. Whatever the motive, Machell was considerably miffed by the extinction of his one chance at fickle immortality. Prosperity made her début and departed. Aurora was incorporated as a village in 1863 and as a town in 1888 when its population rose close to the two thousand mark, only to drop again at the turn of the century.

Aurora had five water-powered sawmills: Lloyd's, Appleton's, Irwin's, Cosford's and Phillips', the Franklin Flour Mills on Wellington Street west and a tannery. The main occupation in the surrounding area was farming, grain and livestock.

Of the local families the Appletons, with a farm on Yonge Street opposite where St. Andrew's College now stands, were for many years among the most prominent in the grain trade.

The coming of the railway to Aurora in 1853 had been a great help in bringing the anticipated prosperity. "Wheat and other grain was teamed to the market from points twenty miles and more distant. Lines of loaded grain waggons would stand from the Franklin Mills (later Baldwin's) to the railway station. At the corner of Yonge and Wellington street the rival grain buyers would stand all day testing and bidding for the loads. The hotel yards would be filled with farmers' teams."[105]

As in the other towns, the hotels profited handsomely on such occasions. One of the best known hotels of the time was the McLeod Hotel on the corner of the property where St. Andrew's College for boys would be built in 1926, a long way from its early beginnings on the old Macpherson estate in Toronto.

And the way of the world there was the farming way, with local industry geared to the needs of the farmers. Nelson and Andrews' grandly named Aurora Carriage Works on Yonge Street advertised "Sleighs and Cutters,—Spring and

Aurora Railway Station (C.N.R.), Wellington Street East of Yonge —
built by Grand Trunk Railway c. 1890.
Original Station built by Ontario, Simcoe & Huron Railway - 1850s?
Visited in 1901 by the future King George V.

Farm Wagons Road Carts, etc..." with payment in "Wood and Lumber taken in exchange for work."[106] Nelson also did horse-shoeing and in 1898 he took over Mitter's shoeing shop that stood across the street from the carriage works.

The decision, some time after 1880, to admit Manitoba wheat to the Toronto market gradually cut into the business of the local wheat farmers. In 1900 Aurora's "daily average of loads of grain paid for would be about twenty" but by the time of the First World War the good years were past, and soon articles would lament that "little or no grain is shipped out and train loads of grains and feed are shipped in to sell to the farmers who are in the dairy and live stock branches of agriculture."[107]

During the 'nineties times became tougher, there were fewer settlers and many people emigrated to the States. *The Globe* in 1910 took the opportunity to blame rising prices on the state of the roads that were a favourite whipping-boy of the paper, but the problem was much deeper than the muddy, rut-rucked surfaces of Yonge Street's rural stretches. "At present during a considerable part of the year it is extremely difficult for farmers to come into Toronto with loaded waggons, and the result is an indefinite increase in the cost of living, which is high enough under the most favourable conditions, apart altogether from the state of the roads."[108]

As usual when prices go up, any old excuse will do for a peg on which to hang the blame, its validity questionable but the result inevitable. To the farmers, it was the protective tariff on manufactured goods that was at the root of their economic difficulties. When the Liberals who had for so long opposed the tariff came to power in 1896, however, they decided that it was not such a bad thing after all and took it into their policy, so that the Liberal *Globe* had to throw the blame elsewhere.

Whatever happens, economic survival depends very much upon the individual's ability to adapt. Versatility was the essential of successful existence in those days before insurance cheques buffered the hardships of unemployment. Farming habits changing from grain-producing to mixed farming in Ontario, the demands of the markets and the requirement for small-diameter logs—all affected the grist and saw mill businesses, causing both to decline. The milling-boom years of the mid-nineteenth century were soon over.

As the mills took their place among the local historic sites, so the hotels and inns were reduced by the hazards of fire and the 'local options' that ended their days as drinking spots, while improved travelling methods reduced their value as stopping-places.

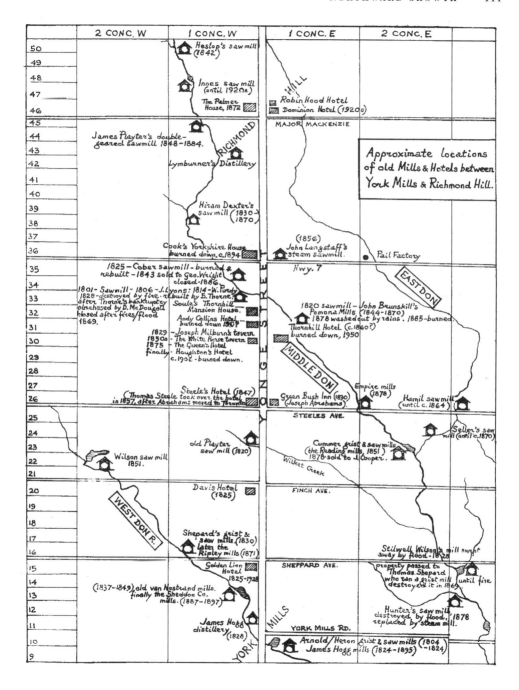

	2 CONC. W	1 CONC. W	1 CONC. E	2 CONC. E

50 — Heslop's saw mill (1842)
49
48 — Innes saw mill (until 1920s)
47
46 — The Palmer House, 1872 — Robin Hood Hotel — Dominion Hotel. (1920s)
45
44 — James Playter's double-geared sawmill 1848-1884 — RICHMOND — MAJOR MACKENZIE
43
42 — Lymburner's Distillery
41
40
39 — Hiram Dexter's saw mill (1830-1870)
38
37 — (1856)
36 — Cook's Yorkshire House burned down, c.1894 — John Langstaff's steam sawmill. — Pail Factory
35 — 1825 — Cober sawmill - burned & rebuilt - 1843 sold to Geo. Wright closed-1886. — Hwy. 7 — EAST DON
34 — 1801 - Sawmill - 1806 - J. Lyons: 1814 - W. Purdy 1828 - destroyed by fire - rebuilt by B. Thorne. after Thorne's bankruptcy purchased by D. McDougall closed after fires / flood 1869.
33 — Soule's Thornhill Mansion House. — 1820 sawmill - John Brunskill's Pomona Mills (1844-1870) 1878 washed out by rains. 1885-burned.
32 — Andy Collins Hotel burned down 1909? — Thornhill Hotel (c.1860?) burned down, 1950
31 — 1829 - Joseph Milburn's tavern
30 — 1850s - The White Horse tavern 1875 - The Queen's Hotel finally - Houghton's Hotel c.1908 - burned down.
29
28
27 — Steele's Hotel (1847) — Empire mills (1878)
26 — (Thomas Steele took over the hotel in 1857, after Abraham moved to Toronto) — Green Bush Inn (1830) (Joseph Abrahams). — Hamil sawmill (until c. 1864)
25 — STEELES AVE.
24 — Seller's saw mill (until c. 1870)
23 — old Playter saw mill (1820) — Cummer grist & sawmills (the Reading mills) 1851 1878 sold to J. Cooper.
22 — Wilson saw mill 1851.
21 — Wilket Creek
20 — Davis Hotel (1825) — FINCH AVE.
19
18
17 — Shepard's grist & saw mills (1830) Later the Ripley mills (1871) — Stilwell Wilson's mill swept away by flood - 1878
16 — property passed to Thomas Shepard who ran a grist mill until fire destroyed it in 1869.
15 — Golden Lion Hotel 1825-1928 — SHEPPARD AVE.
14 — (1837-1849) old van Nostrand mills. finally the Sheddon Co. mills. (1887-1897)
13 — Hunter's saw mill destroyed by flood, 1878 replaced by steam mill.
12 — James Hogg distillery (1828) — YORK MILLS RD.
11
10 — Arnold / Heron grist & saw mills (1804-1824) James Hogg mills (1824-1895)
9

Approximate locations of old Mills & Hotels between York Mills & Richmond Hill.

The village of Thornhill was as prolific with its hotels as it was with its mills in its heyday when business was geared to the needs of grain farmers and travellers. Before the Metropolitan Railway ran its streetcars northward, the nearest railway station of the Northern Railroad was at Concord (Mudville), three and a quarter miles to the west of Thornhill and the old Thompson's Omnibus Line was the transport to Toronto.

And just like the hotel game in the city, proprietors and names often changed faster than a chameleon at sunset. An almost typical pattern of changing fortunes chequered the history of one of the area's oldest inns that was built on Yonge Street in 1829 by the Quaker, Joseph Milburne. Milburne had supported the Reform cause of Mackenzie, but true to the principle of the "quiet people" he took no part in the violent demonstrations of December, 1837. A point that carried little weight when he was found guilty of treason and transported to the convict colony of Van Diemen's Land along with several others who had been more active participants in the rebellion.

After the general pardon in 1843 he went back to his old place of business, but he had none of the success that followed John Montgomery's return to his old haunt. Milburne's past connections, however unremarkable, somehow bedevilled his fortunes, and being unable to get a license for his tavern, he drifted away from Thornhill to go into the tannery trade.

His inn then became John Meek's White Horse Tavern in the late 'fifties. In 1875 it was being run as the Queen's Hotel by the hotel-hopping Henry Lemon. Shortly after that it became Houghton's Hotel, an imposing place with a double verandah, ballroom and stables. The 1906 'local option' bylaw prohibiting the sale of liquor practically put the place out of business and shortly after that it burned down.

Fire put paid to most of the creaking, weather-bleached, clapboard hotel relics from pioneer times—times in which 'gin slings have slewed more than slings of old,' in the opinion of one somewhat disapproving old Methodist doctor in Upper Canada. Whatever the gin may have done for some of the customers, it was the lack of it after the temperance vote that 'slewed' the local hotels and inns that weren't consumed by fire.

The first to go for temperance in Thornhill was the Royal Hotel run by Sheppard and Featherstone until some time in the early 'seventies when it became Mrs. Christian's Temperance Hotel. It stood on lot 32 west side of Yonge Street where it had been built about 1827 for David Soules and was first known as the Soules or Thornhill Mansion House. It was a rather grand building that was purchased by John Thompson for a private home after its fling with temperance. Thompson was involved with the omnibus line and kept his 'bus horses in the ex-hotel's large stables. It ended its days as a nursing home.

The longest-lasting hotel was the Thornhill on lot 30 east across Yonge Street from Houghton's Hotel, somehow surviving the drought when Markham and Vaughan townships voted to 'go dry' in 1906. It may have been started around 1860 by the enterprising Henry Lemon, then it was run by a William Long when Henry took over the Queen's Hotel. By 1909 it was the only hotel left in Thornhill, at which time the owner was Tom Hughes who leased it to a Saunders Findlay.

Findlay bought the place from Hughes in 1920, turned the long-deserted bar room into a billiard parlour and for some years kept a couple of horses that were looked after by an old ostler who hired them out to commercial travellers working the local area. Somehow he kept the place staggering along through the buf-

The old Thornhill Mansion House ~ 1970.

1827? – Built on Soules' Lot 32
1872 – Mrs. Annie Christian's Temperance Hotel
1884 – Bought by John Thompson.
1907 – Bought by Frank Simpson
1946 – Bought by Tobias family.
1970 – Leased as a Nursing Home.

fets of changing times to the almost inevitable end for aging clapboard buildings. It burned to the ground in January, 1950.

Fire also wrote off the Cooks' Yorkshire House soon after its last proprietor, Stunden, moved out in 1894. The next to go in flames, its business evaporated by the 'dry vote,' was the old Andy Collins Hotel just south of the Soules Mansion House. Andy Collins' hotel had a brief moment of notoriety at the start of 1885 along with another Thornhill hotel, known at that time as Captain Symon's, a short distance south of Collins, and which may, in fact, have been the Houghton Hotel. It was in this Symon's hotel that a fatal shooting took place in February, 1885. The newspaper account of the incident described the victim as being "well connected."[109]

He was John R. Arnold whose late father had been a reeve of Thornhill. The young man had met two strangers in Symon's hotel and they all left together to go north to Collins' place where they played cards for money. One of the pair, a man named Westley (or Wesley), ended up owing Arnold two dollars that he refused to pay. An argument and fight followed. Arnold then left by himself to go back to Symon's hotel.

On the way he met Frank Hoff (Huff) of a local shoemaking German family. Westley and his companion, Stewart, followed Arnold and Hoff to Symon's and another argument started there in the bar. In the course of a brawl that has had a variety of versions, it would seem that Hoff for some reason—possibly a bad, or drunken aim—whopped Stewart over the head with a stick, although Westley was making most of the racket.

Stewart then pulled out a revolver and with an equal lack of target selection shot not Hoff but Arnold in the head. That brought a sudden end to an otherwise petty dust-up. Westley and Stewart cleared out of the hotel fast, but they were arrested shortly afterward. Arnold died twenty-four hours later.

A fair number of Ontario's trigger-happy drunks, dangerously unbalanced criminals and delinquent derelicts were liable to find themselves lodged where Simcoe had once planned a base that would be reached via Yonge Street— at Penetanguishene. That was where Upper Canada's first Lieutenant Governor had wanted to establish a base to guard Lake Huron. This was an idea that was not to be realized until the end of the War of 1812, although at that time the road to Penetanguishene was not fit for travelling and was not to be until 1847.

The small garrison that was posted at Penetanguishene, usually little more

Officers' Quarters, Penetanguishene.

than a lieutenant's command, was gradually reduced after 1832, until the barracks were eventually converted into a public reformatory in 1859. This was hardly the sort of end of the road that Simcoe had envisaged. Penetanguishene, however, remained the northern terminus of Yonge Street as perceived by Dr. Scadding, suitably marked by the Northern Hotel that burned down sometime in the 1940s:

> The Northern Hotel, Penetanguishene
> 	Jos. Dusome, Proprietor.
> Choicest brands of liquors and cigars in the bar.
> Best viands and provisions in the larder.[110]

The Reverend Doctor Scadding, whose father had been Simcoe's estate agent in Devon and came to Canada with his employer, said of Penetanguishene in the 'seventies that it was no longer important enough to require an approach such as the extension of the Yonge Street road that had been put through to it in 1847. Important or not, the village was incorporated in 1875 and became a town in 1882.

By the start of the 'eighties the local residents expected that their town would again become important as a result of the railway development "so surely advancing to the North Shore of Lake Huron."[111] Their hopes were partly realized because with the railway Penetanguishene became the northern jumping-off point for more distant places until the roads to the north were opened up by the automobile age.

Until after the First World War the trains and steamers took a steady traffic of campers and tourists to the North Shore and the picturesque but treacherous waters of Georgian Bay, where the fishing was excellent and the air as sharp and clear as a stable-boy's whistle.

> Parry Sound
>   Byng Inlet
> —AND—
> FRENCH RIVER ROUTE
> By Muskoka & Nipissing Navigation Company's Royal Mail Steamers
> "F. B. MAXWELL"
> (Capt. O'Donnell,) and
> "IMPERIAL"
> (Capt. M. C. Cameron), in connection with the Grand Trunk Railway at Penetanguishene and Midland.[112]

These paddle and propeller steamers made daily and semiweekly trips from Penetanguishene, offering stateroom accommodation and first-rate fresh water fishing along their routes.

Naturally, the hotels kept pace with the tourist boom. The Georgian Bay House in Penetanguishene advertised the "best pickerel and bass fishing on the continent," superb scenery, boating and picnic parties. Some places were almost like clubs. Perhaps the best known resort in the area was the one overlooking the bay, the Penetanguishene Hotel that burned to the ground during the fall of 1916.

The best boost, however, for the old military outpost during the last part of the century came not from Canadian enterprise but from the investment of American capital, a fact that would have put Simcoe into the fits. This capital was used to put up sawmills in the Penetanguishene Peninsula, an area almost entirely wooded with the white pine that was in great demand in the United States at that time.

The lumber boom had the same effect on the population of the area as the 'sixties wheat boom had on that of the Barrie and Bradford regions. Many settlers came into the peninsula in the 'eighties from the States, swelling the populations

A COLLINGWOOD SMACKER.

THE PENETANGUISHENE HOTEL

NORTHERN BELLE

MUSKELLUNGE

THE NORTHERN BELLE

THE NORTH END OF YONGE STREET — SIGHTS AT PENETANGUISHENE—1890s.

in the townships of Tay and Tiny that lay on either side of the Penetanguishene Road to around the five thousand mark in each by the turn of the century, almost ten times the numbers that had been in these places in the 'fifties.

The timber went by rail on the Northern Railroad's 1879 extension between Penetanguishene and Barrie whence it ran to Collingwood and Toronto. From here it was shipped across Lake Ontario to Oswego in New York. As with wheat, however, the boom years were short and by the beginning of the twentieth century most of the good timber had been cut from the region. By 1905 the logging and sawmill business had ended although the wood and pulp industry continued on a very reduced scale. And as the timber went, so went the population.

Nothing ever seemed to stay to make a definite mark or establish a tradition where Time had wiped the footprints from the 'Place of the White Rolling Sands,' the Penetanguishene of the Hurons. Like a Stendhalian 'Rouge et Noir' it had housed the 'black robes' of the Jesuit Order, had heard the curses of the British redcoats of the Line who hated the place and gave it the reputation of the most drunken post in the Empire and it had seen fur traders flitting through in pursuit of fleeting fortunes.

Champlain's interpreter, Étienne Brûlé, whom Parkman called the "pioneer of pioneers," had travelled through the region and is believed to have followed the Toronto Portage to the mouth of the Humber River and Lake Ontario, almost two centuries before Simcoe heard of such a trail.

The main routes of the fur trade had passed by Penetanguishene, but the French voyageurs, who were the legend and the troopers of the trade, came down to Penetanguishene with the British garrison that moved there from Drummond Island in 1828. They did not stay long at the new post, but their place was taken after 1838 by an influx of French Canadians from Quebec, whose migration was encouraged by the efforts of the priest then resident at Penetanguishene.

On either side of the road leading into Penetanguishene there stands a statue of an angel, symbol of the combined contribution of the French and British settlers to the history of the area. It is a mute plea for cooperation and understanding between the two peoples, a plea that had little or no appeal at Yonge Street's southern terminus in Toronto.

Yonge Street, stripped of the military and strategic purpose of its creation, was a mere grey meridian between two poles, two extremes of existence. At the north end was the vivid, wind-blasted, Tom Thomson grandeur of Georgian Bay, to the

The old Hillsdale Hotel ~ Penetanguishene Road.

south was the flat, rail track-fringed shore of Lake Ontario and the slum-hemmed huddle of the city.

Toronto was a split personality of American drive and British sentiment. It was Tory, stridently anti-French, the heart of Ontario's business life and a city that was just beginning to be a polyglot of backgrounds. The countryside was Reform or Liberal, settled and slow-moving, traditional in its occupations, suspicious of the city and 'foreign' ways.

A column in the farmers' newspaper, *The Weekly Sun,* headed "The Retired Farmer," said that "retired farmers are not wanted in the towns. They are looked upon as 'mossbacks' and ignoramuses. Their frugal habits are viewed as penurious and there is no place into which they fit, not even in the churches."[113] It was suggested that they should find a comfortable home in a nearby village.

Farmers grumbled about "Toronto's stock jobbers and land speculators," and crabbed about the "waste [of money] on militarism" and the "Navy Folly" that found favour in Toronto's imperial sentiment.[114] In retaliation, Toronto's *Sentinel and Protestant and Orange Advocate* took a more than dim view of such disloyal opinions and, when the United Grain Growers of Alberta ridiculed proposals for a navy, the *Sentinel* prayed that these people were "settlers of other nationalities" than British.[115] At the same time the *Sentinel* carried warnings from the Premier of British Columbia, McBride, about the "avaricious designs" of Orientals who wanted to come to Canada.

This was when Rudyard Kipling was writing for Canadians his poem about strangers in their midst with alien ways and cultures:

THE STRANGER
(Canadian)

The Stranger within my gate,
    He may be true or kind,
But he does not talk my talk—
    I cannot feel his mind.

The men of my own stock,
    They may do ill or well,
But they tell the lies I am wonted to ,
    They are used to the lies I tell;
And we do not need interpreters
    When we go to buy and sell.

Every cosmopolitan city, however, has a share of strangers within its gates and Toronto was no exception. Even in secluded Yorkville a Salvation Army Immigration Hostel had been opened at 916 Yonge Street. As well there were three Chinese laundries and 866 Yonge Street was a Chinese restaurant.

Downtown in the city's core the notorious Ward, where the Irish had brawled and capered in mid-century, had by the nineteen-hundreds become a noisy, threadbare ghetto of Italians, Jews and more immigrant Irish. There was a Mission to Italians on Elm Street in the heart of 'The Ward.'

By 1911 this area between Queen and College, bounded on the west by University Avenue and on the east by Yonge Street, was densely crowded, a huddle of dark cluttered shops, small dingy restaurants, fruit stalls and pinched little houses. Dickens would have revelled in its colour, its surprises, and its successes. It was just across the road from 'The Ward,' in 1909 that young David Dunkelman rented a small store at 245 Yonge Street. He sold made-to-measure suits for fourteen dollars each and so started a business that spread across Canada as Tip Top Tailors.

The *Globe Weekly* of July 16, 1910, with a complacent and undiscerning tolerance toward these strangers in the city's midst, described 'The Ward' as a "picturesquely foreign quarter,' and made a colourful patchwork out of the ragged reality. "Black-bearded men with sacks of rags on their shoulders and olive-skinned hawkers of ice cream parade the streets, women with earrings and round brown arms stand in the doorways, and rollicking children, with sun-kissed cheeks, and eyes shaded by long dark lashes, take their pleasure in the dust of the sidewalk or the gutter. A little later in the year, when sleep in crowded rooms seems all but impossible, the people of 'The Ward' are astir till all hours, and the Italians amuse themselves by singing in their rich, sweet voices the songs of their faraway homeland, or dancing their native dances to the music of a mandolin or guitar in the open roadway beneath the stars."

This rather grubby extravaganza may have seemed a diverting novelty for Toronto, but any feeling for such conditions as those described was unknown in the countryside. There if any sentiment was expressed it was that of the farmer who said that it was necessary "to get up before daybreak in the morning to get ahead of a Jew."[116] Dunkelman was not exactly the country boy's idea of a success story.

On market day, Saturday, "the farmers could come to town and sit on the main street in their horse and buggies, watching the people go by."[117] More than just the people, they were watching at the same time the passing of an age as the horse and buggy made way for the motor car, whose mechanical reliability as yet made a game of chance out of driving when combined with the condition of the roads outside the city.

The voice of the farming community, after generations of lamentation over the state of the roads to the markets, now discovered a new city-bred menace in the automobile that was damned in much the same way that the streetcars were cursed when they began. Because of their noise "it would never be safe to drive a team" on Yonge Street.

> Turning leading highways into an automobile raceway might help
> to populate the cemeteries. It certainly would not add to the
> number of people living along such highways.[118]

By a devious logic it was argued that the result of good roads would be rural depopulation as more people headed for the city. And, said the indignant farmers, it was nothing short of outrageous that they should have to pay for the upkeep of the roads while automobiles were let loose on payment of a paltry $4 license fee to "tear them apart."

The price of progress has never been popular, especially when it is seen as a benefit to somebody else. The farmers objected as strongly to the way public money was spent as had their fathers and grandfathers who supported Mackenzie's reforms. Wee Mac's namesake, Sir William Mackenzie, whom the little firebrand would have looked upon as a disgrace to the clan, was a popular target for the farmers. The railway baron and his partner, Mann, were blasted as the "modern Oliver Twists,' an "unrivalled pair of grabbers [who] have drawn from so many sources, and under so many names, that it is almost impossible to give a full statement of what they have secured. ...in order to surpass this it would be necessary for Sir William Mackenzie to ask for and receive a subsidy for his Toronto Street Railway."[119]

For those who took to the roads on bicycles it was a whole day's journey from King and Yonge Streets to Newmarket on one of the old 'boneshaker' or 'ordinary' machines of the time, a whole world away from the city and its European ingredients. Out in the slow-moving rural towns the key businesses were the old-established trades essential for farming communities. Many lasted well into the twentieth century and preserved the family-inherited skills from a bygone age—harness-makers, blacksmiths and wagon-makers.

A good example of this was Trench's three-storey factor at Yonge and Lorne Streets in Richmond Hill:

> Wm. Trench—Horse-shoeing—Supply Phaetons, Buggies,
> Carriage, Cutters, Sleighs and Platform Spring Wagons.[120]

After William's death in 1896 his son Thomas took over and kept the factory going until as late as 1924. Finally the automobile that had so much outraged the farmers did for the carriage-building trade what the streetcar had done for the stage lines.

Farther up Yonge Street at Holland Landing until after the First World War the horses still plodded out on the soggy marshes. Their weight was supported on wooden slats under each hoof as they hauled the mowers that reaped the village's sole cash crop in the early years of the century—hay for filling mattresses.

The trade and business centre for the Holland Marsh area, an area that had been described as "a mere ditch swarming with bullfrogs and snakes," was the little town of Bradford that had been incorporated as a village in 1857. It had grown up around two early taverns built on the straggling extension of Yonge Street from Holland Landing to link up with the Penetanguishene Road, Milloy's Tavern in 1829 and Edmanson's in 1839. The railway and the lumber boom spurred Bradford's development after the 'fifties, when Thompson Smith built a large sawmill in the area.

On the road north from Bradford was another tiny hamlet that had its origins in the village tavern, Churchill. In the 'fifties it had been known as Gimby's Corners, or less flatteringly as Bully's Acre because of the local rowdies. However it was most easily recognized by the Church Hill House tavern that had a particularly distinctive sign advertising its presence on the road. The owner of this inn eventually moved to some spot on the Penetanguishene Road, taking his sign with him, but the name Churchill remained with the hamlet.

Apart from the tavern, the best-known place in Churchill was probably the smithy and its associated farm wagons and carriage-building business. This was run for many years by a prominent local Orangeman, Henry Sloan, until his son Wallace took over in 1880. Wallace was a Simcoe County councillor who kept the business in the family until 1909 when he sold out to a Sylvester Reynolds. Reynolds in turn sold it in 1920 to John Selman who managed to keep it going for another ten years, by which time the automobile and highway age had spelled the end for many such concerns.

The most impressive town on the northern road was Barrie. Once a terminus for the old Nine-Mile Portage trail, it provided the link to the southern end of the Penetanguishene Road. In the 'fifties Barrie, too, had been a small town with an old log building that became the Bingham Hotel on the north side of the street leading to the Penetanguishene Road. The Bingham became the Queen's Hotel and was gutted by fire in 1915. The street became Dunlop Street, the first business block in Barrie.

Barrie boomed as a major trading centre for grain and poultry with the coming of the railway. In the 'eighties it was probably one of the best market towns in Ontario. The market started early on Saturday mornings and business was always brisk:

> About 11 o'clock there was still a big gathering, and some brisk clearing of the tables. On the square outside there were eight or nine loads of hay, a great deal of pork, and lamb, but not many potatoes or apples. Inside there was a large quantity of fowl, principally chickens, the packer quickly filling three barrels. Fair prices prevailed, turkeys selling for 16c, which is very low. Butter was not seen in such large quantities as a week ago, but there was ample for the demand. Many bought their goose or turkey for Christmas, reckoning on cool weather to freeze and keep the bird. The day

MARKET BUILDING, BARRIE ~ mid-1870s.
The Market Building was built in 1856 and remodelled in 1877. Mulcaster Street ran northward to Penetanguishene Street ("carrion row") that avoided the hills around Kempenfeldt and connected with the Penetanguishene Road (1848).

was very mild and vehicles all on wheels. It is hoped next Saturday
will see good sleighing.[121]

Some typical prices to be found were:

Butter	28c–30c lb.
Eggs, fresh	45c doz.
Eggs, not strictly fresh	35c doz.
Chickens	11c-14c lb.
Beef, fronts	$12.00 cwt.
Hay	$18.00–$20.00 ton
Potatoes	50c bag

Barrie survived a devastating fire in 1875 and the floods of September, 1890 to
become a large, sprawling town by the turn of the century. A long way from the
'fifties when a Joseph Johnson had traded the old Green Bush, once the Last
Chance Hotel on Blake Street, to John Ashley for a farm in Oro township. The
Green Bush was torn down in 1922.

Expanding successful towns, however, were not all a simple progression of prosperity and bliss, as became very evident in the sudden adolescent sproutings of
Toronto. "Mr. D.C. Murray, of the corner of Yonge Street and St. Clair Avenue, is
considerably dissatisfied with the city's assessment department. While his property formed part of York Township some eighteen months ago his land was assessed at $15 per foot, while his assessment paper for the year 1910 shows the
same land is assessed for $140 per foot, which makes an increase of 933 per cent
in eighteen months."[122]

Whether in the country or in the city, it seemed that, like adolescents, nobody
could be satisfied, there always appeared to be somebody else getting more money or a
better deal. Toronto, however, and all of Canada, soon had to grow up very suddenly,
forced by events that were beyond the control of any Canadian citizen, when at 7
p.m., on Tuesday, August 14, 1914, a notice was posted on *The Globe's* bulletin board
on Yonge Street announcing Britain's declaration of war against Germany.

There were instant processions in the streets, cries of 'God Save the King,'
much cheering and bands playing rousing martial tunes like 'Britannia Rule the
Waves.' It was a splendid emotional binge. On the following day the *Star* carried
a Sun Life Insurance advertisement that urged every man to do his duty—and to
take out a Sun Life policy before doing it. And so Toronto went to war.

CHAPTER THREE

BETWEEN THE WARS

1919-1939

Three terse words, "Armistice is signed," flashed into the Toronto newspaper offices at two-thirty on the morning of November 11, 1918. The Great War was over at last and within half-an-hour the newsboys were hollering the good tidings at Yonge and King Street, while bells, whistles, sirens and horns shattered the city's grey silence. By half-past-three cheers could be head from every block on downtown Yonge Street and by five o'clock people were thronging into the heart of the city "by the tens of thousands."[123]

Bonfires were started on Yonge Street and effigies of the German Kaiser and his son, the Crown Prince, were burned or hung at several places. Bands of children formed up to march through the streets, waving flags and yelling. The great sport was to hurl talcum powder everywhere, causing the only casualties from the celebrations. Movement in the city's crowded core soon became almost impossible.

> Mother, may I go and maffick,
> Tear around and hinder traffic?

The Toronto Street Railway's cars did not run at all during the day. The lack of service was cheerfully ignored for once. In spite of the great press of people, there were no ugly crowd incidents. Only one person, "Mike Bonderviver, a Russian," was arrested for disorderly behaviour, having "run amuck several times in the crowd at Queen and Yonge streets."[124]

Many of the villages north of Toronto held their own celebrations, although Richmond Hill sent a full band in a big truck into the city. The Yonge Street farmers who had complained so bitterly about the automobile in the years just before the war must have had a radical change of heart by all accounts. The papers reported the York county farmers to be "well supplied with motor cars, which were all brought out either to run into the towns and villages or to come into the city" for the armistice rejoicings.[125]

In the best North American fashion, sharp business methods and slick advertising with a jumble of meaningless statistics had pushed the automobile upon farmers as a patriotic investment:

> It has been estimated that five acres of land are required to maintain one horse for a year, and that the same five acres would produce nearly enough food for two people. If 50,000 Canadian Farmers each replaced one horse with a Ford, 250,000 acres would be added to the Nation's source of food supply and enough extra food made available to feed 100,000 people.
>
> Just think what a great service this means to the country at the present time and the benefit to the farmers from the sale of food produced on this acreage.[126]

It may have been patriotic, but it was patriotism of the type despised by Doctor Johnson as being "the last refuge of the scoundrel."

A Ford runabout sold at $475 and a sedan cost $970. The Chevrolet Motor Company of Oshawa had a branch run by George Gooderham and Company at 591 Yonge Street. And at 625-627 Yonge Street on the corner of Isabella was an outlet of the Dominion Automobile Company. Cars and roads were now definitely beginning to displace the railways and the steamboat as a popular way of getting around and about. Said the *Toronto Daily Star*, the "peace celebrations gave the city some idea of how great is the need for automobiles. The absence of street car service brought forth every conceivable kind of vehicle."[127]

A New Age was gusting in behind the gales of war, but like all sudden changes it brought about as much confusion as hope. The children who had paraded so boisterously on Yonge Street would grow up, said the *Star*, "in a new world, with Europe delivered from the fear and bondage of centuries and with vast possibili-

1921 Model T Ford

F.R.B.

After W.W. 1 the automobile came into its own; ~ by 1929 the average number of cars crossing Yonge & Langstaff road "reached 5,792" daily during the summer.
                    Robert Stamp; "Early Days in Richmond Hill."

ties of development for every nation in the world. It will be a time of reconstruction—for a new international order, for a new social order in every country relieved from the terror of war."[128]

It was hoped that science used with "wisdom and energy might remove the curse of poverty from the world." An editorial made a great fuss about "Peace and the New Order;" social justice, not military confrontations, would be the battle of the future as the idealists saw it. The down-to-earth farmers' *Weekly Sun* was only worried about what might happen to butter prices.[129]

Of more immediate concern for the mass of people were jobs and wages. Many women had taken the place of men in the munitions factories and not all were content to give up what had been a fairly well-paying job in the face of a large number of returning soldiers, who expected employment as the least reward for their service. "80 Per Cent. Munitioneers Were Unskilled Laborers," and "About Twenty-five Per Cent of Employed Workers in Toronto Must be Absorbed in Industrial Reorganization," headlined the press.[130] And if that was not worry enough, the cost of living was rising. "Budget of Staple Foods Shows Advance of 23 Cents in Weekly Average."[131]

And just as the War of 1812 had produced a greater anti-American and pro-British feeling in Upper Canada, so there was a John Bullish spirit evident in the wake of 1918. In a speech at Port Hope, the Hon. N.W. Rowell, President of the

Privy Council, told his audience among other things: "Austrians, Russians, Mennonites, Greeks and other foreigners have been brought into Canada in droves. They are not Canadians and never will be. They have always been a source of trouble. They have stayed at home and made big money in munitions plants while our boys have fought in France. I hope that in future no one will be allowed into Canada who is not prepared to assume the responsibilities and the character of Canadians."[132]

This was received with loud and long applause and shouts of, "That's the kind of men we want!" The notion of the "cultural mosaic" was quite worthless as a political ploy in those days.

There were fears, nevertheless, that this prejudice against foreigners might be dangerously aggravated by the returning soldiers whose first concern would be to find a job. What was to be done with these foreigners? A popular suggestion in Ontario at the time was to let them go back to Europe if they could be persuaded to volunteer to return and, if Europe, in its shattered state, could take them. At least let no more into the country was the sentiment of the time. Snorted one disgusted veteran in Toronto, "Look at our Immigration Department. It's allowing the Mennonites to flock into Western Canada, Germans and pro-Germans more than half of them."[133]

> It was at wizz-bang corner, Davisville avenue and Yonge street, yesterday afternoon, where the veteran patients from the North Toronto Military Hospital gather on the seats at the corner waiting for the radial cars. ...said one veteran—"Yes, sir. ... a few men of Lloyd George's type would save this country a lot of trouble. We need men who will not truckle to the corporations and moneyed classes, and yet at the same time save the country from an even worse state—control by the Socialists and foreigners.

Business corporations and private wealth at one extreme and Socialists at the other, they were all suspected by the average Canadian of being a threat to the "world freedom and the rights of little peoples" for which they had just finished fighting.[134]

Democracy was not something which Canadians had ever defined very clearly, but in Upper Canada, at least, they had associated it with the American ideals of freedom and independence. As the country grew in population, however, the scope for freedom and independence would be slowly eroded. Up until the war, the Government had done little, if anything, to curb private wealth, and had shown little interest in social welfare. Now, however, there was a growing demand for action in the public interest. "The State is an institution, not to be worshipped, but to serve humanity and to be judged by service," piped the *Star*.[135]

This rather naïve utopianism found its champion in a strange and complex individual. W.L. Mackenzie King, who became prime minister in 1921, was the grandson of the fiery, democracy-obsessed 'Wee Mac,' the leader of the Yonge Street farmers in the Rebellion of 1837. Wily, wary and Machiavellian, King was a blend of Upper Canada's extremes with a belligerent reformer in his maternal grandfather and a conservative army officer on his father's side. Tory Toronto would always be suspicious of him.

As a University of Toronto undergraduate he had played the rebel role by organizing a students' strike, but his contemporaries somewhat sourly remarked that when the strike took place, King was not to be seen, unlike his grandfather who was in the middle of whatever trouble he could stir up. Whenever possible, Mackenzie King would avoid confrontation. He started out as a social crusader in

"WIZZ-BANG CORNER." – *Yonge & Davisville* – *after the painting by Stanley Turner.*

1897 exposing the abuses of immigrant labour in Toronto's 'sweatshop' garment industry, but he wisely wanted only a gradual approach to social reform. In time this cautious rebel became privately opposed to the idea of a monarchy, believing that it was foreign to the notion of democracy because it had too much power, position and privilege.

King's ideas would have let the government decide what was good for society, a somewhat twisted notion of democracy if ever there was one. As such it did not always sit well with many independent-minded Canadians who, while being a charitable people, were lukewarm to the notion of government-enforced liberality. They might have preferred to exercise a personal choice in the matter of goodwill, but the days of the independent patron of charitable causes were fast coming to an end.

Those sternly successful merchants of Yonge Street, the Macdonalds, Cattos, McMasters and Eatons, had not been a mean lot and had given generously to charities. However, charity of that sort was now being looked upon as an uncertain and demeaning kind of succour for the needy. Levies of funds and their redistribution by a central government authority would become the way of the future, a way that would have a yo-yo style popularity according to the state of the economy.

As the new way of things was heralded, perhaps the most fitting chapter-end to the old way in Toronto was the death of J. Ross Robertson, the proprietor of *The Telegram*, on May 31, 1918. A prominent Orangeman, he was the son of John R. Robertson, the well-to-do Yonge Street dry goods merchant and Highland Scot who claimed descent from Duncan, chief of the Clan Robertson of Struan. The elder J.R. married a Sinclair from Stornoway on the Isle of Lewis in the Scottish Hebrides.

J. Ross Robertson became one of that small but motley number of Scots who loomed large in Toronto's newspaper world. The first being with William Lyon Mackenzie himself, who published the *Colonial Advocate* in the 1820s and, on return from his exile, put out the *Weekly Messenger* in 1855 from the Elgin buildings at 79 Yonge Street. Reformer George Brown, the Edinburgh-educated son of a Scots merchant, began *The Globe* in 1844. Then there was that other Reformer and political maverick, the Hon. William McDougall, a Scottish ex-soldier's grandson whose family's farm was just west and south of Yonge Street and Lawrence Avenue. An ardent reformer like Mackenzie, in 1850 he founded the *North American*, a paper that was more extreme than George Brown's *Globe*, with which it was merged in 1857. *The Globe* became the eventual star of the show and after Brown's murder in 1880 another Scot, Senator Jaffray, took over as its publisher.

Robertson, after an early start on the road to journalism at Upper Canada College, became the editor of *The Globe* from 1863-66 and its correspondent in England from 1872-75. In 1876, at number 57 Yonge Street, he started the very successful *Evening Telegram* that would be the source of his fortune. And what a fortune it was! He gave much of it to charity, founding the Hospital for Sick Children in a private house at the corner of Jarvis and Lombard Streets. In the early 'nineties, a new building was put up on College Street. He supported the first hospital without ever having to ask for any public funds to keep it going and it was rumoured that he gave as much as half a million dollars to its upkeep.

In 1883, as a relief for sick children during the sticky heat of Toronto's summers, he built the Lakeside Convalescent Home for Little Children on Lighthouse Point, Toronto Island. In 1916 it burned down. 1916 was also the year when, in the style of the proud Highlander, Robertson refused the offers of a knighthood and a senatorship. His example did much to encourage charity in others, such as Captain Turner who ferried the sick children and their helpers to and from the Island all summer free of charge. It was a last great rally to the cry of 'Noblesse Oblige.'

The time had come for the old Scots merchants and business princes to whistle "Auld Lang Syne." The Edwardian Age, with its sophisticated elegance and risqué raffishness, its comfortable middle class stability and its blind confidence in the future, had gone with the winds of war. It had ended, finished like the passenger pigeons that were once so plentiful about Yonge and St. Clair. By 1923 there was a standing offer of $1,000 for a pair of the birds alive.[136]

The unrest at the start of the New Age was brief. The discontent brought about the United Farmers' government for Ontario in 1919, ousting the Conservatives who had ruled without a break since 1905. In 1923, however, the Conservatives were back again under Howard Ferguson, launching into the brief boom of the years between 1923 and 1930 when the interest in social experiments diminished and few people cared about what happened abroad. Fun was the thing. The spirit of one woman reveller on Armistice Day who whooped that "now it's all over, and the day has come when you can do as you like and go as you please," summed up the new mood.[137] For many people that was about as far as democracy went. And, as might be expected in times of prosperity, social reformers could whistle for their dinner.

Toronto the Good was concerned mainly with keeping up its respectable image. The Toronto newspapers of 1923 said harsh things about the behaviour of youth in America where mindless flappers and clerks made up the audience in New York's theatre houses.[138] And they rejoiced that young Canadian women did not behave like their American cousins who smoked, danced, flirted and frittered away their time at the movies that did nothing to improve their minds or their habits. For the record, Toronto schoolteachers happily reported that their students generally were free from the alarming habits of illicit smoking and carrying-on. Whatever lapses there might be south of the border, there need be no fear of any cracks in Toronto's bastions of morality. Even if that were the case, things would not last that way for very long. Nothing could withstand the appeal from mass communications and advertising, and from popular entertainment.

The myopia of respectability somehow spares society its shortcomings as old eyes spare the aged from their wrinkles. The city already had its fair share of distractions that could make no claim to the improvement of minds and morals. Several of these harmless diversions had their beginnings on Yonge Street where Toronto's first movie had been shown in 1896 at Robinson's Musée near King Street. In 1899 two turn-of-the-century theatre promoters, Jeremiah and Michael Shea from Buffalo, started a vaudeville theatre at 91 Yonge Street between King and Adelaide. Jerry and Mike then moved to the more spectacular Shea's Vaudeville at the southeast corner of Victoria and Richmond Streets in 1910 and later it was given the more dignified name of the Victoria. Shea's on Yonge Street became the Strand Theatre that was run by Alexander McGee at the time of the First World War. The biggest Shea venture, the Hippodrome on Bay Street across from the old City Hall, was opened during the first year of the war. Sound movies—the 'talkies'—were shown there in 1929, and the place lasted until 1957.

Another well-known movie and vaudeville theatre to appear before the war was Loew's on Yonge just north of Queen Street. On a floor above the theatre Loew's created what was to have been a triumph of vaudeville, but in fact became its memorial. This was Loew's Winter Garden that was opened on February 16, 1914, but doomed from the start to be a curio like some Edwardian relic. The Winter Garden had arrived at the end of an age, too late to be adapted to the new ways.

The Winter Garden was closed in 1928, killed by the sound movies of that year, when the first somewhat incoherent, 'talkies' were run at the Uptown Theatre on Yonge Street below Bloor. Both the Uptown and Loew's theatres have

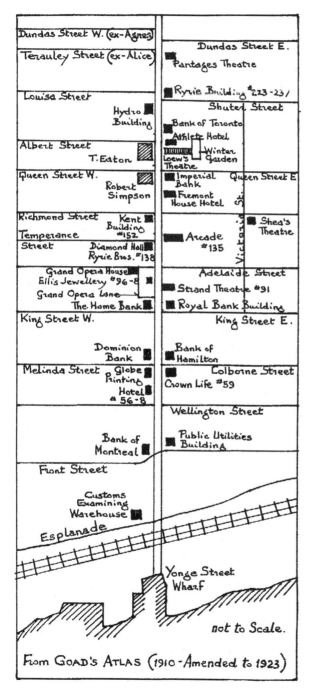

From GOAD's ATLAS (1910 - Amended to 1923)

lasted through the heyday of the 'thirties and 'forties and into the present with Loew's at 189 Yonge Street first becoming the Yonge 'skin-flick' movie-house and then the much grander Elgin Theatre in 1978.

The Winter Garden continued to stand for many years as a decaying memorial to the past, like Miss Havisham's 'Statis House' in *Great Expectations*. Dim, dust-speckled shafts of light filtered in to touch the brass and velvet trimmings, marble stairways and gas-jet foot-lights. Silence hung heavily from the age-blackened ceiling and balconies and the grime-stiff ropes of the back-drop hoists stretched, taut and uncreaking from half a century of disuse. A hand-cranked projector completed the study in Edwardian still-life.

The resurrection was slow in its coming. There was a brief enthusiasm for re-opening the Winter Garden in the years following the Second World War when Loew's considered renovation and 'Honest Ed' Mirvish, the National

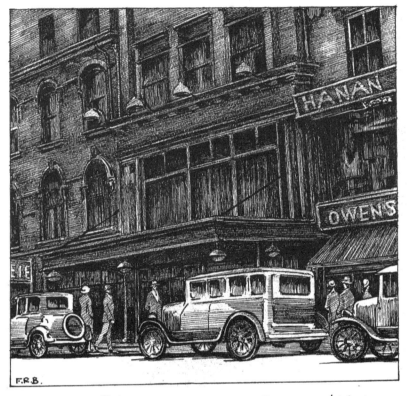

The Strand Theatre on Yonge between King and Adelaide Streets — demolished in November. 1928.

Ballet and the Canadian Opera Company all looked at its possibilities. It would be the end of 1981 before the Winter Garden and Elgin Theatres and a large collection of vaudeville scenery were purchased by the Ontario Heritage Foundation for the creation of a live theatre complex. In the following year both theatres were declared to be National Historic Sites.

In 1987 the federal and provincial governments contributed five million and six million dollars respectively toward the estimated twenty-nine million required for renovation and the construction of the complex was begun. Finally, in December, 1989, the grand opening of the Elgin and Winter Garden Theatre Centre took place.

Through the boom years, through the gloom and doom of the 'thirties' depression as a thousand city jobless were being put to work on outlying farms and through the grim 'forties, the cinemas churned out a steady stream of romance, fantasy and the funnies to provide a diversion. Laugh and grow fat; the movies easily put paid to Toronto's burlesque that had been described as being little more than "salacious humour and slapstick comedy."[139]

Wartime prohibition in Ontario dealt the last blow to the dives and the taverns and some Yonge Street hotels like Philo Lamb's on the southwest corner at Adelaide. The movie house haunts of the new age soon replaced them in numbers and frequency along Yonge Street's city length from downtown to the borders of North Toronto. Nowadays a rollcall of the names would sound like an echo down the lane of memory, a nostalgic reminder of what was popular in the 'thirties and took people's minds off the dreary reality of the times. The old-familiar Loew's on Yonge Street across from Albert Street featured Myrna Loy and Clark Gable in the romantic 'Manhattan Melodrama.' The thriving Uptown provided a lot of hearty laughs with George Burns and Gracie Allen in 'Many Happy Returns.'

The spirit of America invaded Toronto through the entertainment waves, a wonderful Disney world of unreality. Theatre chains cashed in on the new craze and proliferated along Yonge Street as the hotels and taverns once had done. Cinema houses offered a welcome relief from the hot city summers with the "new cooling systems—cooled with water washed air, and polarized air," for thirty cents admission. At Yonge and Gerrard Streets the National showed 'No, No Nanette,' and 'Romance in Manhattan' with Ginger Rogers. Above that were the Victoria at 641 and the Embassy at 654 Yonge Street. Near the Uptown at Yonge and Bloor Streets the York had Wallace Beery in 'West Point of the Air.' Celluloid corner was at Yonge and St. Clair with three theatres in its vicinity; the Hollywood, Queen's Royal and the Beverly. In Davisville the Oriole was showing Bing Crosby and Joan Bennet in 'Mississippi.' Eglinton had two cinemas, the Capitol at 2492 and the Circle at 2567 Yonge Street. And on the city's fringe at Bedford Park, north of Lawrence Avenue, was the Bedford at 3301 Yonge Street.

Although some Torontonians were afraid that there was a bit too much of an 'all-American' influence in these shows, they were generally pretty harmless stuff. Even with the changing postwar standards, however, some of them ran whisker-close to the censor's blue-pencil line. 'Biography of a Bachelor Girl' and 'Baboona' at the Beverly were aimed at the low end of the 'flapper' set. They were certainly not meant for the Old Folks at Home.

Any account of entertainment in Toronto must include the story of the publicity-shy but very successful theatre owner Ambrose Small who vanished from the city without any trace on the night of December 2, 1919. This tightfisted, dapper little man from Bradford had made a fortune out of his chain of Ontario vaudeville-melodrama houses. The foremost of these was the Grand Opera House that stood just off Yonge Street at 11 Adelaide Street West and which had been acquired by Small in 1903.

The old Grand was opened in 1874 at a time when Toronto houses were "crowded to repletion" for shows featuring Lisa Weber's troupe of burlesque girls, 'The Blondes,' in their production of 'Lucretia Borgia.' In 1879 it was badly damaged by fire, but reopened in 1880 to stage 'H.M.S. Parliament,' a Canadian burlesque adapted from Gilbert and Sullivan's 'H.M.S. Pinafore' and performed by E.A. McDowell's Company. The performance was not kindly reviewed.

The Grand was redecorated for the 1895 opera season at the prompting of North York's O.B. Sheppard, manager there for many years and later of the equally well-known Princess Theatre. His wife was the granddaughter of John Montgomery, Mackenzie's Rebellion-famous tavern-keeper.[140] Another Sheppard edited *Saturday Night* in a room behind the Grand in the 'nineties. He was E.E. Sheppard, a colourful character who looked like a motif for Sandeman's wines—flowing cape, plug hat and high boots in grandee style affected after a short visit to Mexico.

In the same year that the Grand was refurbished, Small made several improvements to his

F.R.B.

The Grand Opera House at 11 Adelaide Street, just west of Yonge, and its owner Ambrose Small.

"The least that can be said of Mr. Sheppard's management at "the Grand" is that it has been spirited. During his supervision have appeared Miss Neilson, the late Mr. Sothern, Mrs. Rousby, Genevieve Ward, Mapleson's Italian Opera Company, Sarah Bernhardt, Mrs. Langtry, Mary Anderson, Dion Boucicault, Laurence Barrett, Henry Irving and Company, Tom Keene, Modjeska and a number of lesser dramatic stars." : (Toronto Past and Present; C.P. Mulvany; 1884) own vaudeville theatre in the city, the Toronto. Ambrose Small, age 53 when he disappeared in 1919, was a diminutive, dollar-dazzled rip whose Irish Orange up-bringing—although his father had been Catholic—did not prevent him from marrying a Catholic German of a well-to-do family that could provide the funds to boost his ambitions. Money stuck to Ambrose like feathers to a tar barrel. He also had a rakish taste for chorus girls, like Balzac's bourgeois Matifat "passioné pour les actrices." His affairs with them were carried on in a hidden room that he had built into the second floor of the Grand and he usually showed his apprecia-tion by giving the girl a box of chocolates. Thrift far outclassed romance on the Small scale of values.

This parsimony-shrunken shadow of a boulevardier disappeared after a down payment of one million dollars sealed the $1,750,000 sale of his theatre chain, including the Grand, to a Montreal company. He was never seen again and a popular rumour of the time was that he had been disposed of in the Grand's fur-nace. For many years the mystery surrounding his fate kept Small's name alive in Toronto and made him the object of endless gossip and speculation. The Ambrose Small who emerged from the jigsaw of tales seems, in all, to have been a devious sort of fellow and nobody's fool. Amby Small was a true-blue Mick-on-the-make—true blue, that is, the dollar-swift Yankee business credo that was a part of the American contribution to Toronto's heritage, the quick insight that entertainment was big business and big bucks.

A dazzler of the American business firmament, in the chain store galaxy, was Frank Winfield Woolworth whose wife, Jennie Creighton, came from a log cabin background in Picton, Ontario where she had worked as a seamstress. This bizarre commercial Caesar, work-obsessed and fearful of losing so much as a pen-ny's value, had started his chain store empire with a small variety store in Penn-sylvania in 1879. He expanded his business into Canada in 1912, but before that his cousin, Seymour Horace Knox, had opened a Five and Dime Store on Yonge Street just north of Queen in 1897.

In that same year was demolished the Agricultural Hall that had stood since 1866 on the northwest corner of Yonge and Queen Streets where the old Sun Tavern had once been. When a new building was put up, P. Jamieson who had opened his Palace Clothing House in the old Agricultural Hall during October, 1883, continued his outfitting business there until 1910. In 1910, S.H. Knox's Five and Dime was moved into the Jamieson premises.

Yonge and Queen still kept the image of the commercial parvenu's corner, brash and popular. Knox's and three other companies, Charlton, Kirby and Moore, merged with Woolworth's in 1912 when the Knox store on the corner became the first Woolworth store in Canada. This was also the first retail business to allow the handling of goods by customers, an added twist to the old Eaton line of cash and no credit. When F.W. Woolworth died in 1919, Hubert Parsons of Toronto took over the presidency of the company.

Woolworth's sales were not of novelties but the necessaries of daily living, the requirements of Cinderella-housekeeping: mops, buckets and pails, pots, pans and enamel cookware, buttons, bobby-pins, mothballs and mousetraps, with a brief nod to vanity in hair ribbons. Cheap goods and cheap help made the business go, but in time, changing styles and the pseudo-elegance of 'department store modern' items of merchandise doomed the variety store in the city. The idea of the Five and Dime was on the wane in the 'thirties. By the 'seventies the slightly tawdry regality of the old Woolworth's red and gold décor was giving way to the cooler, classless tone of the blue and white metal panels of the Woolco department stores. Early in June, 1979, the Woolworth store at the corner of Yonge and Queen Streets closed its doors after almost seventy years of business there.

Yonge and Queen was undoubtedly the popular corner in the 'twenties, although the postwar prophets were sure the day was "not very far distant" when the corner of Bloor and Yonge Streets would be the new centre of the city.[141] For conservative Torontonians, however, *the* Corner was still at Yonge and King Streets. Woolworth's, Eaton's and Simpson's were all very well, but fashionable customers still patronized the King Street shops.

There was Catto's, of course, and Michie's and bracketing Yonge Street were Murray-Kay's furnishings that took in the Murray store at 17-31 King Street East and the Kay store at 36-38 King Street West. Murray's had an impressive floor-walker who paraded the premises in a frock-coat with boutonnière. W.A. Murray and John Kay Carpets had merged in 1910. The heir to the John Kay Company, old John's grandson, Lieutenant John Kay, M.C., died at the end of the war from pneumonia following a bout of the flu and in 1923 the business was sold to become Petley and Murray-Kay.[142] During the depression years the John Kay Carpet Company became once again the name of the firm and it lasted in business at 462 Yonge Street until the 1980s.

And on the south side of King just west of Yonge Street was *the* restaurant—McConkey's—that had come a long way from its beginnings on the less exotic reaches of Yonge Street in the 'seventies. It had a Palm Room for the afternoon tea that was the Empire's sustaining ritual, "first we'll have our tea, and then we'll fight the French"—with Mrs. McConkey as the deputy vicereine. By the early 'twenties, however, the restaurant was slipping into the shadow of the eventual eclipse by its rival, the King Edward Hotel Company that bought John Catto's King Street property in 1922, when Catto moved back to Yonge Street.

It was at McConkey's, in 1908, that a group of literary enthusiasts proclaimed the formation of the Toronto Arts and Letters Club, a flicker of culture on the fringe of Yonge Street's darkness. As with its few elegant houses, Yonge Street had but a passing nod for culture, with the Conservatory of Music established by Dr. Edward Fisher in 1887 at Yonge and McGill Streets. In 1912 the Ontario College of Art was incorporated and located at the corner of Yonge and College Streets.

In general, King Street was the focus for commerce in cultural pursuits. Perhaps the earliest venture on the Yonge Street commercial scene was when R.S. Williams, a leading manufacturers of musical instruments, hung his large tin sign of the "Big Fiddle" over a small store at number 144 in 1856. Four years later he moved on to number 206, taking his sign with him. The Williams' business of manufacturing violins and brass instruments removed to Oshawa in 1888 after taking over the Canada Organ and Piano Company. A considerable collection of musical instruments was donated to the Royal Ontario Museum by Robert Williams, the last addition being given in 1936.

The best known manufacturer of musical instruments was arguably Heintzman & Company. Theodor Heintzman started his own piano-making business in Toronto at 105 King Street West in 1866; a business that would spread music retail stores across the country. The family had a very brief association with Nordheimer that claimed to be "the oldest piano company in the Dominion" dating back to a store on King Street East in 1844.

For several years perhaps one of the most familiar signs for "ye olde firme" was the huge advertisement spread on the wall of the Heintzman Company building that dominated the east side of Yonge Street just above Queen from the 1930s to the early 1970s. The business was eventually sold to the Sklar Company in 1981.

A late arrival on the scene was the firm of Gourlay, Winter and Leeming, established in 1890 as piano distributors at 188 Yonge Street. The company started manufacturing pianos in 1904 and branched out across Ontario, but ended in bankruptcy in 1923. Threat of closure was also a shadow in which the Morris

Piano Company flirted with various partners until its eventual demise in 1924, by which time it was the firm of Morris and Karn. The company, based in Listowel, Ontario since 1892, had showrooms early in the century in Toronto at 276 Yonge Street.

Yonge Street may never have been the beau monde, but sprouting along it were names that would coalesce in Canada's most prestigious jewellery firm, Birks, by whom even the smallest purchases continue to be wrapped in a regal style long out of fashion. The firms of Ryrie in the Diamond Hall at 134-138 Yonge and Ellis at 96-98 had, by the 1930s, become Birks-Ellis-Ryrie at Yonge and Temperance Streets, having gradually displaced both the Kent Brothers at number 168 and Murphy's at 141 that had for so long held sway on the Street.

The old dry goods Scots names were gradually disappearing, although Eaton's and Simpson's seemed entrenched and Catto remained for a while. But there were newcomers who would last to establish an equal mark, like Frank Stollery's gents' furnishings at 790-4 Yonge Street at Bloor. Dineen's, the hatters, became successful furriers. And in the 1930s at the corner of Yonge and Adelaide Streets was another elegant firm, famous since 1837—Holt, Renfrew and Company, 'Furriers to Four Generations of Royalty.'

The age of elegance, however, faded almost before it had begun.

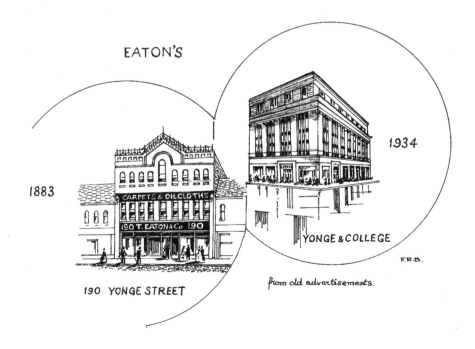

EATON'S

1883

1934

CARPETS & OILCLOTHS

190 T. EATON & Co 190

YONGE & COLLEGE

F.R.B.

190 YONGE STREET

from old advertisements.

Toronto got little more than a passing handclasp from the age of Edwardian elegance. There was a brashness about the city that defied the subtleties and muted distinction that flavour style, but the brashness was a part of the drive and energy that were essential if the exuberant hopes of a brave future for Canada were ever to be realized. The style could come later, when the confidence had been established for its growth. And when it came, it would have to be something very different from what Simcoe had hoped for, with his dreams of creating an hereditary aristocracy along English lines in Upper Canada.

That sentimental English Tory, scruffy old Doctor Sam Johnson, standing at the threshold of eighteenth-century England's Industrial Revolution, had rumbled in sour suspicion that, "when the power of birth and station ceases, no hope remains but from the prevalence of money." And there was lots of that in Toronto, enough to purchase all of the semblance, if not the substance, of regality.

Real estate deals, land speculation and business initiatives spurred hopes and won wealth in prewar Toronto for those who were willing to invest capital and take risks. The greatest plunger of all, of course, was Major General Sir Henry Pellatt, C.V.O., D.C.L., described as having been a Canadian soldier, financier and philanthropist, the builder of Casa Loma in which he never lived.

An old boy of Upper Canada College, he made and lost a fortune in his lifetime, started some of Canada's main industries and was one of the country's small group of important financial leaders for nearly forty years. In 1879, at the age of twenty, he set up the Toronto Electric Light Company that got a one-year franchise in 1883 along with the Canadian Electric Light and Manufacturing Company to supply lights on different streets in the city. The first arc lamp was put up at the corner of Yonge and King Streets in 1884, the same year in which the Canada Electric Light and Manufacturing Company's franchise was cancelled.

From then on, the cry was 'press on regardless,'—and press he did. When Toronto, along with other municipalities, signed a contract with the Ontario Hydro-Electric Power Commission that had been instituted in 1906 to provide power, the Toronto Electric Light Company refused to sell its plant. The Company remained in competition with the local Hydro until 1922.

The list of companies with which Sir Henry was involved was a roster of Canadian businesses: The Crow's Nest Pass Coal Company; Dominion Steel Corporation; Mining Corporation of Canada; Brazilian Traction, Light and Power Company; São Paulo Tramway Light and Power Company; Toronto Railway Company; Canada Steamships Company; Dominion Telegraph Company; British

American Assurance Company. This tycoon of Toronto's business world was knighted in 1904.

When the Canadian West was being opened up at the turn of the century. Sir Henry bought all the stock that he could in the Northwest Land Company and came out of it with close to four million dollars. He gave a great deal of money to his beloved military, particularly the Queen's Own Rifles, of which he was Colonel, and that was affiliated with the Buffs of the British Army. He gave steady support to the Grace Hospital, donating a surgical wing to it in 1903. In 1901 he gave $25,000 to the endowment fund of Trinity University.

It was land speculation that finally unhorsed him. He incorporated three Land Development Companies between 1911-12; British Colonial Land and Securities, Toronto City Estates and Home City Estates. His prewar speculations were on a staggering scale, but with the First World War investment practices changed drastically to the detriment of men like Sir Henry. During the war, Victory Loans and War Bonds were repeatedly floated with much patriotic drum-beating and high-flown speeches. These Loans sparked an uncontrolled wartime boom that sent prices steadily up and made life difficult for a lot of people. Canadians were putting their money into war bonds and very little, if anything, into the purchase of land or into house building. This decline of interest in housing meant in turn that the Land Development Companies were left holding land that nobody wanted.

Sir Henry Pellatt was saddled with a bag of properties that had scarcely increased in value. When the Home Bank in Toronto near the northwest corner of Yonge and King Streets declared bankruptcy in 1923, one of its largest debtors at the time was the stockbroking firm of Pellatt and Pellatt. It was the beginning of an end for the big speculators, with added pressure coming from the postwar tax law that taxed land itself and not just the buildings on it, so squeezing the Land Development Companies even more. A further pinch for many was the Dominion Income Tax introduced by the Borden Government in 1917.

Land—what had at first been given away so freely by Simcoe to those he imagined loyal to the British cause against republicanism, and which had been so highly prized by those 'freeman of the soil' from America, who farmed north along Yonge Street was now worth much. Much more than its original owners and developers could have ever imagined. But the greatest, grasping official paw could still reach out and snatch back whatever amount of land might be needed for the plans of bureaucracy. In 1911 town planning powers had been given to municipal authorities by the City and Suburbs Plans Act of the Province of Ontario. A Department of City Planning and Surveying was created in 1930 for Toronto.

Just before the war, the City had put pressure to sell their land on some of the old families that were settled on Yonge Street beyond the northern fringes of Toronto. Between 1911 and 1913, the elderly descendants of pioneering families that had settled north and east of Yonge Street and Langstaff Road, James and William Russell, Nathan Chapman, George and Walter Quantz, sold out to City offers for their land. One man, David Boyle Jr., the postmaster of Langstaff from 1902-27, refused to sell.

The City gave him Hobson's Choice. He could either sell his two hundred-acre farm for $39,000 or have it expropriated if he continued to refuse. Some time in 1914, Boyle's farm and large brick home at the northeast corner of Yonge and the Langstaff Road were expropriated to become the start for the seven-hundred-and ninety acre Langstaff Jail Farm. In May of that year, Boyle moved to Homewood Hall in Thornhill. Such was the fate of a parcel of land that had originally been a part of the much larger Crown grant to Abner Miles, the founder of Miles' Hill that later became Richmond Hill.

Suburban developers were prepared to offer better deals for farmland that could be used for housing schemes. On the city fringes, at what is now Yonge Street and Lawrence Avenue, the Lawrence brothers from Yorkshire, England had obtained large tracts of land on both sides of Yonge Street in the early 1800s. By the middle of the century, Peter had a two-hundred acre farm on the northeast corner, John had three-hundred acres on the southeast corner and Samuel was on the northwest corner. Jacob had a tannery whose location has been variously placed at the southwest or the southeast corner, although his land lay to the north of Peter's on the east side.

Their farms, market garden and tannery were healthy investments, but they were also very attractive to real estate developers. The particular outfit that had an eye on the Lawrence property's prospect was the Dovercourt Land Building and Savings Corporation. The president of this concern was W.S. Dinnick, who had come out from England about 1890, and saw golden opportunities in the area of North Toronto for building speculation. While his brother developed the Glebe Manor Estates in Davisville, W.S. in 1908 acquired the three-hundred acre farm of John Lawrence at the southeast corner for $90,000. His idea was to turn it into an area of high-class suburban residences. The name of Lawrence Park Estates had about it an up-stage and down-county ring that would appeal to those with squirely pretensions.

The postwar land tax, however, put paid to the whole notion, squeezing the Dovercourt developers in a financial pinch, so that their unsold Lawrence Park properties had to be unloaded at an auction held there in 1919. Dinnick himself had a substantial home on Lawrence, not far east of Yonge Street.

Dinnick at one time also lived in Bedford Lodge near the northeast corner of Yonge Street and Teddington Park Avenue, a house that was occupied by a succession of successful Toronto merchants. The land on which the Lodge stood was first bought in 1887 by Robert Dack of the shoe firm and the house was built in 1903. Teddington Park Avenue came into being in 1912 when Dack subdivided the land for residential development. W.S. Dinnick and later Frank Stollery of the gents' furnishings followed Dack at Bedford Lodge. The house itself was eventually torn down in the spring of 1978 to make way for half a dozen new houses. Across from Teddington Park Avenue, on the west side of Yonge Street, was the one-hundred and seventy-seven acre farm and home on the estate of Alfred St. Germain, a Toronto newspaperman. He died in 1908 and the present St. Germain Avenue is named after him.

And just south of there, between Woburn and Bedford Park Avenues, and stretching from Yonge to Bathurst Streets, was the old 1870 Metcalfe house and its estate. These were bought in 1889 by the Ellis wholesale jewellery family of Yonge Street. Around the turn of the century, when the development bug was beginning to itch investors, W.G. Ellis decided that a Company town nestling in feudal snugness on his estates would be a good thing. Consequently, he created 1,500 lots on his estate for that purpose, in spite of the fact that the local council in 1898 had firmly squashed this idea of a factory being built there by the Ellises as the hub of their 'town.' By 1908 the Ellis subdivision was well under way, and a few years later houses were going up on what is now Ranleigh Avenue. In 1926, Ellis sold his own house, 'Knockaloe,' to the Roman Catholic Archdiocese of Toronto. The building at the end became a four-room school before being demolished in 1945.

W.G. Ellis was a leader of the North Toronto Ratepayers' Association that campaigned for better roads and transportation and was also a power behind the North Toronto secession movement between 1915 and 1920. Even *The Barrie Examiner* and *Barrie Saturday Morning* on April 30, 1920 was speculating on the outcome of this move by North Toronto to break away from the city:

WHO SHALL DECIDE THE QUESTION OF SECESSION
NORTH TORONTO OR THE CITY AS A WHOLE?
Opinions at the City Hall appear to be divided even yet as to if the
people in North Toronto really want secession, and Alderman
Hiltz has even gone so far as to declare that if a vote were to be
taken at the present time the majority would be against secession.
Others have stated that if Yonge street were cleaned up the whole
question would be settled without a vote being taken.

Cries of secession are usually only a less blatant way of howling 'gimme.' Come wars, depressions or disaster, one thing had remained constant through the cycles of weel and woe, complaints about Yonge Street and transportation. With cars for all becoming the tangible evidence of democracy in North America, the demand for more and better roads mounted and would not be stilled as the volume of traffic increased. It was also a very difficult demand to meet with a quick response, because the scale of future problems that had also to be considered was almost impossible to foresee. You may take or leave the gypsy fortune-teller at the fair, but that sort of thing won't do for city planning.

Better roads were the high price of the great infatuation with the automobile, and the roads that had been built one-hundred years before for the strategic designs of a distant government could not be suddenly adapted to satisfy popular requirements. Money, as usual, was the rub.

When it was suggested at the end of 1921 that Yonge Street should be widened before double-tracking it for a speedier streetcar service, an improvement popular with the North Toronto vocalists, advocates of the idea said that the major portion of the costs should be borne by the city. At the beginning of 1922, Yonge Street north of old Yorkville was to be widened to eighty-six feet from its original width of sixty-six feet from lot line to lot line. This was to be done, in one instance, by taking land on the east side from Shaftesbury Avenue as far as Heath Street. The property owners along the way and "citizens at large would each pay one-half of the cost of the work" of widening the road.[143]

That brought the opposition bouncing out of its corner. Property owners said that the City should pay seventy-five per cent of the cost, but the City authorities were adamant and the cost-sharing remained on a fifty-fifty basis. The optimists predicted that within the year Yonge Street would be "an 86-foot highway from the CPR tracks to Heath Street."[144] Road-widening, however, was to be an expensive and destructive process that would eventually threaten many old land-marks and divide people into progress-at-any-price and save-our-heritage groups with lunatic fringes in each of them.

In 1922 it was pointed out that if Yonge Street in the older part of the city was to be widened, then the Imperial Bank building at the southeast corner of Yonge and Bloor Streets—where the width was not much more than twenty feet—would have to be torn down. The streetcar had become paramount and the old would have to make way for the pathway of progress, with a sometimes scant regard for the casualties along the way.

In 1896, when the M.S.R. track had been put through Richmond Hill, the house of Colonel Moodie, who had been killed in his attempt to warn of the march on Toronto in the 1837 Rebellion, was moved south to the adjacent lot to make way for a spur track. In the summer of 1931, when Yonge Street was being widened to one hundred feet in North York, Willowdale United Church had to be torn down. It had been built in 1856 to replace the original log cabin church erected on that site when Willowdale was known as 'Cummer's Settlement.'

And new ways of living, while not immediately popular, were at least begin-ning to make an appearance and be greeted with some doubt and tooth-sucking by the older generation. The single-family home, the private house, had always been at the heart of Canadian living, the focus of society. To own a house and land was the great North American Dream, the immigrants' vision, particularly for those who had come from feudal, tenant-farmed Europe. The appeal of apart-ment-style living would gradually seduce many people away from that ideal. After the war the apartment-village of Summerhill Gardens mushroomed where once had stood Summerhill, first the home of Charles Thompson, who took over the old Weller Stage line, and later of Larratt W. Smith the lawyer. The Smith home was torn down in 1914.

The old Steele's Hotel that had stood since 1847 on the northwest corner of what is now Steele's Avenue and Yonge Street was another familiar landmark that would eventually give way to the twin demands of automobile and housing. Thomas Steele had acquired the place in 1857 and ran it until his son John took over in 1877. Like most hotels at the end of the nineteenth century its main rev-enue came from the bar-room until the local option of 1906 ended even that. The hotel became a Hunt Club house and then a tea-room called the Green Bush. Around 1910 Steele sold the hotel to a Mr. Spink for a private home.

The building was bought in the 1930s by T.R. Collins and the front half was

The Green Bush Inn (once Steeles Hotel) – Yonge & Steeles – c. 1910.

demolished 1970.

moved to a spot farther west on Steeles Avenue. What was left of the north wing was later torn down and the old driving shed became the foundation for a duplex that faced onto Yonge Street. The corner space, made vacant when Collins shifted the front portion of the house, was taken up by a gas station and, when business soared, the duplex was demolished to provide more land for the station.[145] The avenues for progress that had seemed to open up in the 'twenties, however, became for the most part cul-de-sacs by the 'thirties.

Before the great Crash of 'twenty-nine, there was a cautious optimism that encouraged hopes of more suburban growth in the areas lying to the north of the city along Yonge Street. An indication of that attitude was the creation of the municipality of North York as a separate entity from York Township on June 13, 1922. It took in the region that ran from the city limits through York Mills to Steeles Avenue. Its largest community was made up of the long-settled farms and their homes that fronted on Yonge Street, the districts of York Mills, Lansing, Willowdale, Newtonbrook and Steele's Corners. At the same time Yonge Boulevard was constructed at the city limits by the Department of Public Highways. In 1929 the first Hogg's Hollow bridge over the Don River Valley at York Mills was completed and Yonge Street joined the Yonge Boulevard on the west end.

The American-style enthusiasm for more efficient travel ways was always tempered in Toronto, however, by a Scots caution, 'gang warily.' The turn of the century had been a great carnival of innovation with gadgets and inventions of varying degrees of usefulness. On what was, perhaps appropriately, April Fool's Day, 1898, an advertisement had appeared for 'The First Canadian Autocar,' brainchild of Mr. Alfred St. Germain, the man who owned the estate in North Toronto. This autocar, it was claimed, would be able to cope with the steep grades on Yonge Street between Toronto and Richmond Hill and it would be the first combined passenger and parcel van capable of seating twenty-five persons, "The first in Canada if not on this continent."[146] And, as they say, the first shall be last, because no more was heard of the idea.

In Toronto itself, as early as 1910, the city authorities had received tenders for "the construction and operation of an underground railway along Queen street from the City Hall to Sunnyside."[147] This proposition was regarded as being too radical at the time and innovators had to continue to concentrate their efforts on ways of improving roads and the existing system of public transportation by streetcar. And if there was ever an inexhaustible subject for complaint, then the streetcar was it.

The Toronto Railway Company did nothing to help matters by refusing to extend its streetcar fare beyond the old limits of its 1891 franchise. If the city wanted to expand then that was not their problem, said the Company's officials. As a result, there were several streetcar lines run by the city out to the suburbs, but they made travelling expensive for people with any sort of distance to go. Subways would have provided the best form of rapid transit northward, but the public had voted against that idea. What was popular, however, was the proposal for public ownership of the streetcar services; a proposal for which support had been mounting steadily in proportion to the dissatisfaction with the Toronto Railway Company.

The Toronto Railway Company also owned the Toronto and York Radial Railway and in 1904 it had purchased the Metropolitan Railway. As the city expanded well beyond its old 1891 limits, so new lines were built out to the annexed areas, but operated by the city as the Toronto Civic Railways and not by the Toronto and York Radial Railway. The city, as a result, was running nine separate transit systems by 1920, each one having its own particular fare and no transfers. The whole structure of transportation in Toronto was well on the way to becoming too costly and unmanageable.

By the end of the First World War, the Company had allowed its tracks to deteriorate into a deplorable state of dilapidation because of its reluctance to part with any money for their upkeep. Money, it must be admitted, was not so easily come by at that stage of the game, because the automobile was starting to do to the streetcar services what the streetcar had done to the horse-stage lines—undercut them; victims all of progress. More and more people were using cars that could now be mass-produced and run on cheap gas. The Yonge Street road from Toronto as far as Barrie had been vastly improved, so that it could have been no surprise to anyone that the Toronto and York Radial Railway's service from Toronto north to Jackson's Point on Lake Simcoe was losing money. The cash for upkeep and repairs was simply no longer available.

The city and its transportation system had reached such a size as to be too great for effective operation by a privately owned franchise. On the first of January, 1920 the people of Toronto voted in favour of the city authorities taking over the Toronto and York Radial Railway when its franchise ended in September, 1921. And in 1920, as if to emphasize the state of affairs, there was a streetcar strike in Toronto. The Toronto Transportation Commission was formed on the first of September, 1921, and after two years of this public ownership the various routes had been amalgamated to provide one fare covering the whole city with transfers between routes. In 1923 the first concrete two-lane pavement was laid with the streetcar tracks on one side, or in the centre of the road. Solid-tire, double-decker buses were a novel feature when introduced by the City on some of its routes in the fall of 1920.

Nevertheless, it could almost be guaranteed that one thing would not change, the public's enthusiasm for grumbling. "The first fifteen minutes of waiting for a street car up town is the worst. After that you get acquainted with some of the others, and can pass the time away cursing the Commission."[148]

The facts of existent improvements and the hopes for continued progress could not, however, be denied—and were very evident in contemporary comments:

> It is quite a change for the residents [of the Hill area of St. Clair Avenue] to ride down town on a "Bay" car instead of an "Avenue Road" car. They are finding the service down Bay St. speedier than the old Yonge St. route, although the scenery for some of the route is not so attractive. ...

> One real improvement is the cross-town line on St. Clair. Cars are

now running from Caledonia Road to Yonge Street. The "shuttle" service from Avenue Road to Yonge Street is eliminated, the residents hope, for ever.

That St. Clair Avenue is destined to be one of the great commercial thoroughfares of Toronto is becoming more and more apparent.[149]

The east-west thoroughfares were now receiving increased attention as Toronto again felt the surge of growing pains and a buoyant postwar optimism. "Yonge Street has enjoyed a great prosperity because for years it was a thoroughfare crossing unbroken the full length of the city. But now Bloor comes into power, and already it is being driven through to tap Dundas St. at Islington on the west."[150]

With such developments in anticipation, the CPR in 1915 had built its one million dollars' North Toronto station at Yonge Street below St. Clair Avenue. This location was used as a passenger depot for only a few years until 1927 when the new Union Station was opened at Front Street on the city's southernmost edge. The vision may have been cloudy, but imperceptibly the centre of the Toronto cosmos would shift away from King and Queen Streets.

On either side of Yonge Street, in the old downtown area, there was little evidence of hope or of prosperity, rather there was utter squalor. The ever-infamous Ward to the west and Moss Park to the east of Yonge Street were described in the report of a Committee on Housing as "the worst slums of Toronto."[151]

> THE WARD
> In this district we find a greater number of commercial and industrial buildings than in Moss Park. Some of them such as the T. Eaton Company on the one hand and the junk dealers of Elizabeth, Centre and Chestnut Streets on the other, require the extensive use of trucks which clutter up the streets and make it very unsafe for children. ...
>
> ....To some modern painters the district has appeared artistically worthy of preservation—at least on canvas. But to the eye of the layman it presents a heap of tumbled down buildings, streets bordered by collapsing shacks, junk yards and storage sheds. Trees have been driven back to the north and west portions of the district leaving the remainder a very barren land. It is an unpleasing picture."[152]

For the first time, housing was becoming a serious concern of the Dominion and Provincial governments. Given the conditions described above, it is hard to believe that anyone could discover advantages in them. Nevertheless, there were some earnest social soothsayers who declared the Ward's children to be sturdier than those of the well-to-do. They attributed this spurious, slum-engendered health to open air, sleep and 'wholesome" food—even grimy air being considered better than the stuffy confines of a house, no matter how splendid the mansion might be, and stale buns, no doubt, better than cake. The children of the middle-class, it was suggested, were overmuch cosseted. Inhabitants of Rosedale, incensed by such half-hatched opinions and the implied slight to themselves, dismissed the supporting statistics as ridiculous and unreliable.[153] The pundits would seem to have confused gutter-toughness with good health.

Just as Yonge Street had early been divided into 'two nations'—rural folks at one end and townspeople at the other, so there existed in the town the denizens of the slums with very little and the well-to-do with every benefit at their command. The playgrounds for the poor were the back streets. They might be able to kick an old ball around, but not to play the golf and tennis and cricket of the more comfortably-off. Money made available sports, country clubs and country-fresh air for the fortunate as they wished.

Running at least retained its democratic flavour from the days of the Ancient Athenians. Cross-country runs, however, were favoured more by the country house set then by the lads of the village. In 1924 the Challenge Cup for the annual Cross-Country Race was presented by HRH the Prince of Wales on October 16 at Whitmore's Farm on lot 82, Aurora.

The vicinity of Aurora and Newmarket provided a desirable rural setting for the country homes of some of Toronto's successful families. Mr. Timothy Eaton, the grandson of founder Timothy, would make his home in Tara Hall on Yonge Street just north of Aurora. And south of the town was Hazelburn Farm, where the hounds of the Toronto Hunt, begun in 1843, were kennelled. Hazelburn belonged to Mr. Aemilius Jarvis, the Master of the Hunt in the 'thirties.

Aemilius Jarvis, a scion of 'old family' Toronto and of the Irvings of 'Bonshaw' north of Newmarket, represented a social atmosphere as rarefied and different from that of the Ward as fresh country air from the staleness of the slums. His ancestor the Hon. Aemilius Irving of the British 13th Dragoons, squire of 'Bonshaw,' had been wounded at the battle of Waterloo. Aemilius Jarvis followed in this military tradition of an upper class. He won the Military Cross in 1918,

BONSHAW ~ The Irving Estate, north of what is now
Davis Drive, Newmarket.   c.1860.

when a lieutenant in the Royal Canadian Dragoons, for recovering and burying the body of a fellow officer before his company retired from its position.

The son of Commodore Aemilius Jarvis of the Royal Canadian Yacht Club, he had been educated at Ridley College where he was caption of the football and cricket teams and, at seventeen, was the junior tennis champion of Ontario.[154] This golden image, a modern version of the "parfit knyght," was badly tarnished in 1924 when the Jarvises were involved in a lawsuit over some supposed sharp practice in bond deals which were negotiated with the Ontario government and the Home Bank. The bank, certainly, was by that time a byword for crass incompetence and negligence, having been forced to close in 1923.

E.C. Drury, who was Premier at the time of the deals, always believed that gentlemen of the style of the Jarvises could never have been wittingly guilty of any dishonourable act or deceit. A portion of the public, however, made cynical by the war, was not so convinced and argued that an acquittal of the Jarvises would be clear evidence of 'one law for the wealthy, another for the poor.'

In the 'thirties the privileged sailing and yachting world of the Jarvises was centred in the Royal Canadian Yacht Club. Toronto's exclusive RCYC had its mainland station at the very bottom of Yonge Street, close by the Canada Steamship Lines' old docks. The foot of Yonge Street had by then been extended some

The Toronto Waterfront, early 1920s before the landfill operations.

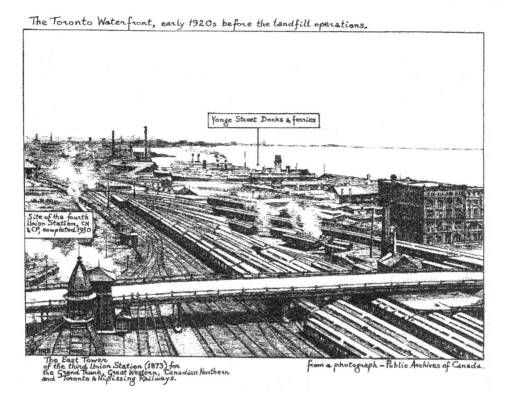

Yonge Street Docks & ferries

Site of the fourth Union Station, CN & CP, completed 1930

The East Tower of the third Union Station (1873) for the Grand Trunk, Great Western, Canadian Northern and Toronto & Nipissing Railways.

from a photograph – Public Archives of Canada.

eleven hundred feet into the bay as part of a nineteen million dollars' development plan of the Toronto Harbour Commission in the mid-'twenties.

The Canada Steamship Lines' Yonge Street sheds were demolished in 1927 and, as part of the new look on the waterfront, subway bridges were built at Yonge and Bay Streets with the 1929 Viaduct Agreement. These bridges finally made it possible for cars to reach the harbour without having to cross some sixteen railway tracks. Also in 1929 Colonial Airways began an airmail service between Toronto and Buffalo, New York. Their amphibious, twin-engine plane, the Neekah, would berth at the ramp of the Harbour Commission's terminal at the foot of Yonge Street. The terminal was closed in 1932.

Up at the farther end of Yonge Street, on the route to Lake Simcoe, about the only change taking place was a difference in the manner of getting there. The weather-worn, age-grey stucco hotel on the corner of School and Yonge Streets at Newmarket had seen generations of passengers ride up on the old stages and later on the radial railway streetcars to Jackson's Point at Lake Simcoe. In the middle

1926 - Silhouette of Toronto, looking north on Yonge Street from the R.C.Y.C. dock.

The tall landmark in the centre is the Royal Bank building on the n/e corner of Yonge & King; one of the city's earliest skyscrapers.

of March, 1930, however, this streetcar service from the North Toronto terminal at Hogg's Hollow was suddenly discontinued.

The streetcar was then succeeded by a bus service that ran up Yonge Street from the city to Thornhill, Richmond Hill and Newmarket, thence to Jackson's Point. Meanwhile, a local bus service ran from North Toronto to Richmond Hill. This local service lasted no time at all, being replaced in July, 1930 by a reversion to the old streetcar service that was then called the North Yonge Railway.

What had happened was that the City of Toronto authorities had sold the North Yonge transport franchise to the Townships of North York, Markham and Vaughan and to the Village of Richmond Hill. These places then arranged for the Toronto Transportation Commission to supply a streetcar service from North Toronto to Richmond Hill. This service ran until October, 1948 when, in an attempt to save hydro power, the streetcars were once again replaced by buses.

As a requiem, there was a strong movement in Newmarket in 1979 to preserve the very last of the old radial streetcar line's bridges that ran across the Holland River, when the bridge was marked for demolition because it caused floodwater spills over the river-banks.[155]

By the end of the 'twenties the Toronto Transportation Commission had become well aware that public transport was not providing a ride comparable with the comfort and convenience of the private automobile. The latter, it is true, could never be quite equalled, but at least comfortable, cheap and frequent public service might provide an attractive alternative to the car and its growing popular-

North West corner of Yonge and Queen Streets — new streetcar introduced by the T.T.C. in 1938 to meet the challenge from the automobile.

ity. A measure of the increase in motor vehicle traffic—and the number of accidents—was the installation, in 1927, of the first traffic lights in Toronto. Their location does not seem to be anywhere recorded.

The Depression years, while putting a temporary halt to the popular demand for automobiles, also blighted any prospects of readily available revenue for the improvement of public transportation. It was not until 1938 that a new model streetcar was at last brought into service.

There had been depressions enough before 1929 in the eternal business cycle of boom and bust, but this one was on an unprecedented scale, of world rather than regional proportions. As such it was incomprehensible to people whose frustrations and distress from the sudden, unexpected losses of jobs and income threatened the very foundations of society.

Society became a seesaw, precarious and unbalanced. Newspapers still conveyed announcements of teas and dances being given by mothers to introduce their eligible daughters to the social set. Elsewhere there were bankruptcies, hunger and pleas for relief underscored by a large advertisement from the Federation for Community Service's campaign:

> Those who have
> MUST SHARE
> with those who have not
> Every one who can share, must share! Those who
> can give more, must give more.[156]

Another indication of this mounting desperation was the increase in the number of hold-ups of small stores being reported, often where only a young woman clerk was in charge of the premises. These incidents and purse-snatchings were the outbursts of the desperate rather than of the deliberate criminal. The pickings were seldom more than a hundred dollars, although there was always the danger of panic producing a serious crime. Typical was the robbery of Blachford's shoe store at 748 Yonge Street one October evening when two men, one armed with a revolver, tied up the clerk and made off with what they could find in the till.[157]

In a general way, however, the tough times were not as harsh in Southern Ontario as in other parts of the nation. The practice of mixed farming that had been made necessary by the bad years for Ontario grain at the end of the previous century now proved to be a blessing of sorts, because it reduced the dependence upon a single commodity for cash.

In the areas north of Toronto the Depression's blow was nevertheless still relatively heavy in spite of their rural farming base. Estimates of the number of people suddenly unemployed have been put as high as forty per cent of the working population. The dearth of local industries meant a very weak tax base for these rural areas and the land was cheap in comparison with city properties. The verdict on many of the small communities lying north along Yonge Street was, "too many homes and too few industries for a balanced tax assessment."

In Aurora, for example, there was some manufacturing in a small way with the Sisman Shoe Company established there in 1907. As a business it was pretty much a 'one-man show,' its founder and president being Thomas Sisman who had started out in Markham before moving to Aurora where he died in October, 1933, after more than fifty years of shoe making. The Collis Leather Company was also established in Aurora some four years after the start of the Sisman operation.

The only large factory thereabouts was the Fleury plough works occupying an entire block on Wellington Street just west of Yonge Street where the business was begun in 1859. In an attempt to weather the winds of adversity it was merged with Fleury-Bissell of Elora, but finally foundered around 1939.

The collapse marked the end of what might have become a pattern of long association, as rural manufacturers went the way of the hotel-keeper, miller and blacksmith. W.H. Fleury had at one time owned the old Doan Hall property, an honoured local landmark just north of Yonge and Wellington Streets in Aurora. The land there had been sold in 1846 to Charles Doan by Hanner Playter of the early Loyalist settler family. Now all the old values of land and work and family were being shredded by the winds of a frightening change.

South of Aurora, in the farming village of Richmond Hill, the familiar Trench's carriage works closed in 1924. One blacksmith, James Hunt, managed to stay in business until some time in the 'twenties on the west side of Yonge Street just south of the old Langstaff home at Hall and Dunlop Streets. True to its motto, 'en la rose je fleuris,' Richmond Hill had a flourishing rose-growing business in the greenhouses of John H. Dunlop, with a shop in Toronto. This lasted from 1913 to 1930 when Dunlop died. In 1934 the greenhouses in the village were taken over by H.J. Mills, Limited, at that time the largest rose-growing concern in Canada.

The next village to the south, Thornhill, saw the first wave of a new trend, the commuters, arriving just before the First World War. This northward surge was given an increased momentum by the Depression. The cheaper land and lower taxes in the districts north of Toronto attracted people from the city, where they could no longer afford their homes and were forced to move out.

House building was almost at a standstill in the 'thirties, when the building trade was described as being "the most backward of all industries." And while there had been a marked improvement in the roads during the boom years of the 'twenties, there were now fewer cars to be seen on them. The bubble of progress seemed suddenly to have burst.

The great strength of the rural towns and villages during hard times was their strong sense of community, the legacy from their pioneering, farming origins with their memories of past hardships shared and overcome. Country newspapers did not need to run advertisements to encourage or remind people to look after their unfortunate neighbours. There was also, perhaps, more of an effort to preserve dignity in misfortune. Nevertheless, work programs were started everywhere, in town and country, for those on relief, in an attempt to cushion the demoralizing effects of unemployment.

In Toronto, 'Community Gardens' were started in the summer of 1935 to employ the jobless by giving them garden plots where they could grow food for themselves and their families. It was reckoned that in this way nearly one hundred acres of land were cultivated by a jobless army of more than one thousand men. One block of these garden plots was located at Yonge Street and Eglinton Avenue.

Another scheme in 1934 provided work for Dutch immigrants on relief at Holland Marsh at the Lake Simcoe end of Yonge Street. The reclamation of Holland Marsh was enthusiastically endorsed at that time as a major achievement in husbandry. Its drainage system was then being designed to develop the soil for crops such as celery, lettuce and carrots.

Professor W.H. Day of the Ontario Agricultural College at Guelph, Ontario predicted that when the whole of the Holland River Valley marsh was brought under cultivation it would "produce enough celery and lettuce to feel all of Canada."[158] The expectations may have been exaggerated, but the Dutch immigrants did develop the Marsh's potential for growing vegetables into a very creditable output.

Every human endeavour has its limits and charity is no exception to the rule. The tug-of-war between the have and the have-nots is eternal and unresolved, a perpetual slither in the mud of reality. By the summer of 1935 complaints about the cost of relief schemes and payments were being loudly voiced by the providers.

> The tremendous cost of this relief work makes it imperative that something be done to weed out the impostors.[159]

The unemployed organized themselves into hunger marchers or 'trekkers' to march from Toronto to Ottawa to demonstrate their plight. A great parade, with the Union Jack required by law at its head, formed up at Queen's Park for the start of the 'trek' in July, 1935. The average 'trekker' in this On-to-Ottawa crusade had in no doubt about the general public's scant sympathy for his cause; an attitude in part caused by his admitted reluctance to take up offers of farm jobs which he regarded as exploitation and a trick to spoil the effect of the march to Ottawa.

Muttered *The Globe* on July 15, 1935: "It would be much better for the "hunger marchers" if they accepted the advice of candid friends that they are making

HOLY TRINITY
CHURCH
1930s.
Consecrated 1847.
Trinity Square off the
west side of Yonge and
just below Queen.

In 1845 an anonymous gift of £5,000 was given to
Toronto — £3,000 for the building of a church and
£2,000 to invest as a stipend for the rector.
In 1894 the donor's name was disclosed; Mrs. Swale,
the wife of a clergyman in Little Yorkshire, England.

themselves unpopular with the public, which is being taxed almost beyond endur-
ance for their support."

At the end of the month the mayor of Toronto gave in to local demands and
announced that the physically fit single men on relief would either help the farmers or be cut off the relief rolls.

The unchecked downward slide of the Depression had by this time ended the
Conservative government of Premier George S. Henry (1930-1934) and the Tory
régime in Ontario. Baffled by the unfamiliar winds of the time, Henry could set
no firm course and his use of troops and 'baby tanks' during a strike in Stratford
in the fall of 1933 was an unwise reaction that advertised his insecurity.

His successor, the Liberal leader Mitchell Hepburn, showed no doubts or hesitation. He was a master of the use of pizzazz and personality in politics and prom-
ised a new deal for Ontario. 'Mitch' Hepburn, the good ol' farmer from the back
concessions, was publicly scornful of his predecessor's experience of farming on
the Henry family farm at Sheppard and Woodbine Avenues where great-grandfather Henry Mulholland had settled in 1806.

Hepburn could play dirt farmer rustic or pal to the industrialist; a man for all types. His interest was entirely in his Province of Ontario, particularly the farmers of the back lots and he had little concern for the federal scene. This, of course, was a reflection of the general drift toward 'regionalism' that had started after the War and strengthened during the Depression years.

If he is remembered at all it is usually as being anti-labour, although his government did enact laws that raised wages and improved working conditions. What finished Hepburn was his continuous opposition to the federal Liberal government of Mackenzie King; and King neither forgot nor forgave. Professor Creighton called Hepburn the "chief critic and detractor of the Dominion."[160]

Much of this, of course, was a symptom of the confusion of the times aggravated by the unshakable Depression that had extinguished the brief flame of optimism that blazed in the wake of the War. The hungry continued to turn to places like the Yonge Street Mission that had been established in 1896 opposite Walton Street. And there was still a lack of work enough to give presence to the Ontario Single Men's Unemployment Association. In August, 1938 the police expelled fifty unemployed from the Queen's Park bandstand in Toronto. The *Globe and Mail* admitted that "the fact is that we are a long way from a solution to the relief problem."[161]

In the best human fashion ideals still flourished in spite of the almost universal pessimism, as evident in a speech by Dr. E.A. Hardy of Toronto, a Past President of the Canadian Teachers' Federation: "In our two nations [Canada and U.S.A.] there is a steady interweaving of the threads of racial characteristics, ideals and traditions into a pattern of citizenship which should ultimately transcend anything which the world has known."[162]

He described the popular term "melting pot" as "fundamentally inaccurate."

Set against that vision, however, was the fear engendered by the actions of Japan in the Far East and such headlines as, "Chinese Flee before the Japs"; a fear that prompted alarm that there could be designs upon Canada's empty northlands. This was given expression by Mr. W.D. Albright, the Superintendent of the Dominion Experimental Farm Substation, Beaverlodge, Alberta: "Only too well may the yellow race adapt itself [to the Canadian North] and surely it will do so, by peaceful penetration at first and then by conquest if the white race neglects nature's motto, 'use or lose'."[163]

At times it would seem that there was a greater concern over what the Japanese might do than over what was happening in Europe. The alarm bells there were ringing stridently, echoing in the *Globe and Mail*'s headlines, "Drive to Rid

Berlin of All Jews Continues with Unabated Vigor," and "Goebbels Spurs Nazi War Against Jews."[164]

As might be expected, some prophecies would prove to be false. Franco's chances of victory in Spain's civil war were "deemed slim" in the summer of 1938, and elsewhere Hope deafened ears to reality; "Czechs Doubt Germany Will Try Invasion." Attempts by Britain's Sir John Simon to warn Hitler of serious consequences from his actions were treated with "scorn" in Berlin.

Canada stirred uneasily. It was proposed to make a joint RCN/RCAF survey of Anticosti Island for a potential Air Base to defend the St. Lawrence River. The *Globe and Mail* reported that, "Canada's Armed Forces Stage Mimic War as End to Training" at Camp Borden on August 29, 1938, and a day later, "War is Prophesied With Canada Involved." For good measure a 'Red Scare' was thrown in with police in Toronto reported to have found a "huge increase in Communist ranks."

The prognosis was, to say the least, gloomy. However, while the manoeuvres at Camp Borden may well have been the first to be held by the Regular Army since the War, at the same time the survivors from that war staged the greatest Veterans' Reunion since its end. It was a tremendous tamasha. Although a year's grace would remain, the celebrations were a last great revelry before the conflict, the ball before Waterloo, a magnificent display of camaraderie. They also served as a grim reminder of the price that had been paid.

Yonge Street was the maypole around which the revelry revolved, probably the most colourful roistering in the entire history of the Street. To fully appreciate the spirit of the shenanigans the eyewitness accounts in the newspapers provide perhaps the best descriptions:

> At the height of the festivities at Queen and Yonge Streets two
> Third Division men opened a florist's shop right in the middle of
> the intersection. Holding aloft two very bedraggled daisies one of
> them cried, "Genuine French marigolds, one dollar a bunch."

and

> ... at Yonge and Queen Streets early Sunday morning ... a dozen
> veterans were seen to pick up a baby car and carry it bodily to the
> door of a department store ... but the midget car was just a little
> too wide so they left it on the sidewalk.

and

A couple of cars were parked just below the Yonge and Richmond Intersection and their proud occupants, both veterans of the 1st Division, sat back contentedly drinking their beer and protecting(?) themselves from possible head injuries by holding above them a battered and smashed umbrella.

As a grand finale,

Downtown Toronto actually went wild early this morning as more than 10,000 veterans and civilians gathered along Yonge and King Streets, lit bonfires at numerous intersections, paralyzed traffic, shot dice on the street, pushed one grand piano into a street car

F.R.B.

"And the old boys from Toronto fall into step"...
The Globe & Mail, 02 August, 1938.

"For two full hours, under the rays of a broiling sun, that gallant, impressive, yet somehow pathetic cavalcade passed by, backs arched, arms swinging as one, chins held high."

" Line after line they came, and there was something in the way they walked that stirred up a fever of pride in the thousands upon thousands of old and young who lined the route of march." [along Fleet Street].

" One soldier turned his sightless eyes as he passed the reviewing stand. Guiding him was his trained dog. Not once did his step falter."

" Colorfully dotting the parade at several points were Indian veterans in full regalia. Some carried peace pipes, a few war-drums."
The Globe & Mail, 01 August, 1938.

To accommodate the veterans, "French Village" was set up in the East and West wings of the Coliseum in Exhibition Park.

and burnt another, and otherwise boisterously but jovially rang
down the curtain on the 1938 Canadian Corps Reunion.[165]

At the end, the crowd broke into three large groups; at Yonge and Queen
Streets, Yonge and Richmond and Yonge and Adelaide Streets. Up and down
Yonge Street they surged. A quickly improvised crowd control was established by
sending four fire trucks to race up and down Yonge Street in an attempt to prevent groups from massing at any one spot. It was not successful. Eventually the
civilian content in the crowd outnumbered the ex-soldiers by ten to one according to one estimate and there were signs that an ugly situation might develop.
The arrival of extra police finally restored order and calm.

The casualties resulting from the merrymaking were, "3 dead, 302 hurt in 71
automobile accidents and 37 collapses"; a tolerable record for such an occasion.
For their patience with the Reunion crowds well-deserved praise was accorded to
the police, described by one source as "probably the most maligned group of indi-
viduals in the city."

While the police received general acclaim, the roads continued
to be a perennial source of complaints and criticism. "Horse and
buggy type streets" were blamed
as the cause of Toronto's traffic
problems. At the time of the Reunion one writer suggested that
"at the rate weekend accidents
are piling up, it may become the
duty of another body of veterans,
the survivors, to organize to make
the roads safe for motoring."

Sometime in 1916 Yonge
Street had been included in the
stretch of highway that ran from
the city to Severn Bridge at the
northern end of Lake Couchiching; the route numbered Highway Eleven. In 1936 the Ferguson

POINT DUTY at YONGE & QUEEN STREETS ~ 1930s.

Bordered on the east side by Yonge Street and on the
south side by Queen Street was the notorious St. John's
Ward or, more simply, "The Ward".
1830s ~ Known as "Rebels' Corner."
1870 ~ Rowdies' Corner for "the batch of rogues who nightly
            assemble" there.
Eaton's (1869) & Simpson's (1872) Corner.
1880 ~ Young women "of no good intentions" reported to be
            strolling on Yonge Street below Queen.
1912 ~ First Woolworth store in Canada.

Highway that had been opened in 1927 to run north from Lake Couchiching was incorporated into Highway Eleven and Penetanguishene, the original terminus envisaged for the Yonge Street Road, became merely an offshoot from the new line of advance.

In the summer of 1939 some new restrictions on drivers were introduced. The speed limit on Yonge Boulevard from the city limits to Harley Avenue was set at 30 mph. And a $50.00 fine would be levied for the somewhat loosely phrased charge of 'careless driving.' Grumbled one disgruntled citizen, "it has taken the Department of Highways two years to come to a decision regarding these restrictions," generally considered to be long overdue.

When two cars collided a mile south of Aurora on Yonge Street now Highway Eleven in the summer of 1938, seven people were injured. At the same time a headline stated that "Over Score Are Injured on Highways," and a year later without numbers or statistics came the bald assertion, "Too Many Slain by Autos."[166]

By the time of that last pronouncement, however, a field with greater potential for killing than Highway Eleven was evolving. In spite of the steadily mounting tension in Europe during 1939, the blindness of Hope continued to cloud the reality. Lord Beaverbrook, a Canadian success story in England, still believed war to be "unlikely." And a recent arrival in Canada, Baron Adolf Christe-Lomnitsky, a great-grand-cousin of Austria's last Emperor on his way to take up farming outside Toronto in August, 1939 dismissed Hitler as a "passing phase."

At Lake Couchiching, the end of the original Highway Eleven, an appeal was made by the secretary of the Canadian National Committee on Refugees for Canada to provide a haven for European refugees. He blamed opposition to the idea upon the lethargy and "political dullness" of English-speaking Canadians and a "timid and unimaginative" government.

This came at a time when two thousand Jewish refugees from Czechoslovakia had unsuccessfully tried to run the British blockade of Palestine. The Canadian Jewish People's Committee concurrently protested against the widespread distribution of anti-Semitic literature in Toronto and the rejection of Jewish patrons from hotels in Ste. Agathe des Monts in Quebec. It looked in vain for action from Ottawa.

Then, like the crash of 'twenty-nine another 'Black Friday' shook the world on September 1, 1939. The *Globe and Mail* carried the news in a special *Extra* edition with the startlingly large, mourning-black headline,

NAZI PLANES BOMB POLAND

It was the beginning of the end to peace for Canada, as W.H. Auden introduced it in his *Danse Macabre*,

> It's farewell to the drawing room's civilized cry,
> The professor's sensible whereto and why,
> The frock-coated diplomat's social aplomb,
> Now matters are settled with gas and with bomb.

Much, if not all, depended upon how Britain would react. Across Canada there was still a very strong pro-British sentiment. This had been spectacularly evident in the Royal Tour during the spring of 1939. When King George VI and Queen Elizabeth stepped off the royal train at the North Toronto station on Yonge Street just below St. Clair Avenue at ten-thirty on May 22, 1939, the thousands that were gathered "yelled and roared their hearts out."[167]

Toronto was united in an emotional outpouring of affection for the living symbols of Britain and its Empire as the storm-clouds gathered over Europe. A magnificent military panoply coloured the event: the burnished and plumed Royal Canadian Dragoons; the RCAF band; the naval full-dress uniform that would be obsolete after the Second World War worn by the RCNVR officers in the honour guard; the scarlet, blue and gold of the RCMP. In the afternoon the King would present colours to the Toronto Scottish Regiment and in the evening inspect the Queen's Own Rifles' guard of honour on departure from Union Station, with a royal salute from the 9th Toronto Field Battery. It was a splendid display of pageantry that for the moment hid the appalling lack of an effective force behind it.

The day was perhaps the most hectic one for Toronto since the Armistice and the previous year's Veterans' Reunion. Yonge Street, said the *Toronto Daily Star*, was "converted into a canyon of cheering." At seven o'clock in the morning twenty thousand people had made "sidewalk traffic on Yonge Street within six blocks impossible." After eight o'clock motorists had been prohibited on the street.

As the royal cavalcade passed down Yonge Street from the North Toronto station someone raised a World Peace flag at Crescent Road. Outraged veterans shouted that it should be torn down, but a tactful constable of the RCMP suggested to the man that it would block the view for other spectators and the flag was quietly folded up by its obliging owner.

Overcast skies and a light drizzle could not mar the event. The cars continued down Yonge Street to tremendous outbursts of cheering. The *Globe and Mail*'s reporter, carried away by the moment, eulogized it with a somewhat skewed perspective on Yonge Street's importance in the past:

> It was history that passed through these streets of Toronto, too.
> Madly cheering throngs, perhaps momentarily, saw not the signifi-
> cance of that trip down Yonge Street. But the King rode the way
> that rebels once rode, passed the spot where rebels had once sought
> to wrest from England's kingship the right to rule Canada.
>
> And yet in that King's parade there also rode the Little Rebel's
> grandson. And together they rode across a historic spot, where a
> thousand men and women stood or clung. They rode across that
> corner where, more than a century ago, a skirmish had kept
> Canada for England. ...

The royal smiles, however, did nothing to ease the feud between Mackenzie King
and Hepburn.

In just under four months after the royal visit crowds were out again on the
downtown streets, but for a reason much less joyous by far. Following upon the
German invasion of Poland, Britain had declared war on September 3rd. A general mobilization had been ordered in Canada, although the government seems to
have been in some confusion over whether or not this was a good idea and implied that the military had acted too hastily. Certainly the country was woefully
unprepared. The Army in its training exercises had been reduced to using dummy
tanks and substituting lengths of piping for mortars.

Britain went to war on September 3 and on the 4th "anxious, news-hungry"
crowds jammed the sidewalks outside the newspaper offices waiting for press re-
leases. The crowds were "tight-lipped" and grim in sharp contrast to the cheering,
processions and bands that had greeted the news of war's declaration in 1914.
They knew all too well the toll to be exacted.

One week later and more black headlines delivered the dreaded but expected
blow:

CANADA DECLARES WAR!

Copies of the Proclamation dated September 10 were carried in the *Globe and
Mail* and the *Toronto Daily Star* on the following day. Again Canada went to war,
but in a more subdued fashion. For those who hitherto had complained about the
menace of automobiles upon the highways there would be some small recom-
pense in the wartime rationing of gasoline.

NOTES

1. *The Daily Telegraph*, October 22, 1870.
2. *The Globe*, April 1, 1875 and March 2, 1872.
3. Ibid, March 30, 1870.
4. *The Daily Telegraph*, September 9, 1870.
5. *The Newmarket Era*, April 13, 1866.
6. *History of Toronto & County of York*, C. Blackett Robinson, Vol. 1, p. 289.
7. *The Evening Globe*, January 19, 1875.
8. *The Daily Telegraph*, July 9, 1870.
9. Ibid.
10. Ibid, October 1, 1870.
11. *The Mail*, March 16, 1875.
12. *The Daily Telegraph*, July 27, 1870.
13. *The Globe*, March 5, 1872.
14. Ibid, February 23, 1872.
15. *The Mail*, April 2, 1880.
16. *The Daily Telegraph*, October 29, 1870.
17. *Toronto Past and Present*, C.P. Mulvany, p. 230.
18. *Toronto, Old and New*, G. Mercer Adam, p. 142.
19. *Toronto, Past and Present*, C.P. Mulvany, p. 230.
20. Ibid, p. 85.
21. *The Globe*, March 31, 1870.
22. *Toronto, Old and New*, G. Mercer Adam, p. 159.
23. *A Merchant Prince*, Rev. Hugh Johnston, p. 138.
24. Ibid, p. 197.
25. *Of Toronto the Good*, C.S. Clark, p. 59.
26. Much of this information was provided by John Catto's grandson, Mr. John M. Catto of York Mills, President of Clifton Cosmetics.
27. For clues to the history of these hotels, see *A Collection of Historical Sketches*, by J. Ross Robertson (microfilm reel No. 2 in Archives of Ontario); *History of Toronto and County of York*, by C. Blackett Robinson, Vol. 1, p. 475; and two articles on "Yonge Street in the Early 60's" by Mr. Harry Smallpiece in *The Toronto Daily Star*, December 18, 1909 and January 8, 1910; *Goad's Atlas, 1890* - Plate 10.
28. *The Globe*, February 20, 1883.
29. *The Colonial Advocate*, April 26, 1827, advertised one Jackes having the Rising Sun, lately Snyder's at Yonge and Dundas—possibly a mistake, because the Sun was at Yonge and Dundas. The Rising Sun, run by Jackson(?) in the 'sixties, was at Yonge and Bloor. There

was probably a connection between the Jackes of the Rising Sun and the Jackes of the Gardener's Arms.

30. Toronto City Directory for 1868,

31. *The Daily Telegraph*, December 6, 1870.

32. *The Daily Leader*, June 9, 1866.

33. *Toronto Past and Present*, C.P. Mulvany, p. 308.

34. See advertisements in *The Mail*, March, 1875.

35. *Toronto Past and Present*, C.P. Mulvany, p. 305.

36. *The Daily Telegraph*, January 12, 1872.

37. *The Daily Telegraph*, January 12, 1872.

38. *History of Toronto and County of York*, C. Blackett Robinson.

39. Toronto Past and Present, C.P. Mulvany, p. 58.

40. *Of Toronto the Good*, C.S. Clark, pp. 71-2.

41. *Mail and Empire*, May 28, 1934.

42. *The Daily Telegraph*, October 21, 1870.

43. Ibid, November 2, 1870.

44. Ibid.

45. *History of Toronto and County of York*, C. Blackett Robinson, p. 286.

46. *The Daily Telegraph*, July 9, 1870.

47. Ibid, November 20, 1870.

48. *Toronto Called Back*, C.G. Taylor, p. 147.

49. *Star Weekly*, July 15, 1922; "Yonge Street's Last Blacksmith Shop in Ancient Tavern Near Bloor Street," by Lyman B. Jackes.

50. *The Globe*, May 24, 1922.

51. *Newmarket Era*, August 26, 1870.

52. *The Christian Guardian*, March 17, 1886.

53. *Victorian Toronto: 1850 to 1900*; Peter G. Goheen, p. 119.

54. *The Liberal*, August 8, 1878, and *York Herald* for 1879.

55. Ibid and Ibid.

56. *The Liberal*, January, 1899.

57. *Toronto Past and Present* , C.P. Mulvany, p. 260.

58. See *Scrapbook Collection* No. 57, Archives of Ontario, and "Some Notes on a Visit to Penetanguishene and the Georgian Bay in 1856," by Elmes Henderson.

59. Material in the Biographical Index Section, "Macpherson, D.L.," Archives of Ontario.

60. *Historical Sketch of the Town of Barrie*, 1884; Archives of Ontario.

61. For Baron de Hoen, see *The Yonge Street Story*, 1793-1860; F.R. Berchem.

62. *The Evening Telegram*, May 14, 1935.

63. Ibid, January, 22, 1927; "Sale of Benvenuto Shows Odd Financial Record:"—When S.H. Janes sold the property to Sir William Mackenzie in 1897, he accepted Toronto Railway stock instead of cash as payment.

64. *York Herald*, October 25, 1888.

65. *The Liberal*, December 15, 1892 and December 29, 1892.

66. See *Scrapbook* - Flashbacks and Window of the Past - Richmond Hill Public Library, Richmond Hill, Ontario.

67. *The Liberal*, July 25, 1895.

68. Ibid, November 5, 1896.

69. *The Globe*, June 23, 1910.

70. *The Liberal*, July, 1899.

71. Ibid, August 10, 1893.

72. *Newmarket Era*, August 19, 1864.

73. *Aurora Banner*, June 17, 1892.

74. *York Herald*, November 20, 1879.

75. *The Liberal*, October 31, 1895.

76. Ibid, October 15, 1896.

77. Ibid, December 20, 1894.

78. *The Globe*, September 14, 1910.

79. "The Toronto General Burying Grounds," by Emerson S. Coatsworth in *York Pioneer*, 1971. ...The Chairman of the board of the Toronto General Burying Grounds in 1876 was William McMaster, who started the plans for the Mount Pleasant cemetery. He is buried there.

80. *Aurora Banner*, February 22, 1896. As an example of how high feelings and loyalties still ran, the *Newmarket Era*, April 8, 1870 had an irate letter written by N. Allan Gamble, who had no time for Reformers. He was then Quartermaster of the 12th Volunteer Battalion and was annoyed because the Corporation of Newmarket wanted the Volunteers' supply of ball cartridge stored somewhere other than the room occupied by the local Fire Brigade. This request, and the fact that Newmarket was in Reformers' country, led Gamble to conclude his letter with the blunt comment that it didn't say much for 'the loyalty of those in power,' nor 'for patriotism of Newmarket.'

81. *Mike: The Memoirs of the Right Honourable Lester B. Pearson*, Vol. 1, p. 11.

82. *The Globe*, June 23, 1910.

83. Ibid.

84. "Incidents in the Life of John Montgomery," by his granddaughter, Mrs. O.B. Sheppard in *York Pioneer*, 1967. John Montgomery spent many years in the old Franklin House that later became the Robinson House—rather ironically, because it was J.B. Robinson who passed the sentence of death on Montgomery. Montgomery died at Orillia in February, 1880, aged 96.

85. In *Scrapbook No. 45*, Archives of Ontario.

86. *The Globe*, October 5, 1910.

87. Ibid, August 15, 1910.

88. Ibid, November 30, 1910.

89. Ibid.

90. Ibid, January 10, 1911.

91. *York Pioneer and Historical Society*, Annual Report, 1908.

92. *The Globe*, August 17, 1910.

93. Ibid, September 15, 1910.

94. Ibid, August 19, 1910.

95. Ibid, December 12, 1910.

96. *Aurora Banner*, February 22, 1896.

97. "Henry Blackstone or How Henry Died," by Ralph Berrin in *York Pioneer*, 1964.

98. In *Scrapbook No. 45*, Archives of Ontario.

99. *York Herald*, February 5, 1885.

100. *The Liberal*, November 15, 1894.

101. Ibid, October 1, 1896.

102. Related by Mr. Boynton of Richmond Hill.

103. *The Liberal*, February 2, 1895.

104. Ibid, August 8, 1878.

105. In *Scrapbook No. 45*, Archives of Ontario.

106. Aurora *Banner*, 1892 editions.

107. In *Scrapbook No. 45*, Archives of Ontario.

108. *The Globe*, December 9, 1910.

109. *York Herald*, February 5, 1885.

110. *The Penetanguishene Herald*, August 14, 1890.

111. Pamphlet No. 32, Archives of Ontario—"In Commemoration of the Visit of the Sovereign Grand Lodge, Independent Order of Oddfellows, and Their Guests, to Penetanguishene, Saturday, Sep. 18, 1880."

112. *The Midland Free Press*, September 6, 1888.

113. *The Weekly Sun*, January 22, 1913.

114. Ibid.

115. *The Sentinel and Orange and Protestant Advocate*, January 30, 1913.

116. *The True Life Story of David James Howard*, Richmond Hill Public Library, 1972, p. 64.

117. "The Nickel-and-dime empire" in the *Toronto Star*, March 3, 1979.

118. *The Weekly Sun*, March 5, 1913.

119. Ibid, June 4, 1913.

120. *The Liberal*, November 8, 1894.

121. *The Barrie Examiner and Barrie Saturday Morning*, December 17, 1914.

122. *The North Toronto Progress*, July 14, 1910.

123. *The Globe*, November 12, 1918.

124. Ibid.

125. Ibid.

126. The *Weekly Sun*, January 16, 1918. Advertisement for Ford cars.

127. *The Toronto Daily Star*, November 12, 1918.

128. Ibid, November 11, 1918.

129. *The Weekly Sun*, January 16, 1918.

130. *The Toronto Daily Star*, November 13, 1918, and November 11.

131. Ibid, November 18, 1918.

132. Ibid, November 13, 1918.

133. Ibid.

134. *The Globe*, November 11, 1918.

135. *The Toronto Daily Star*, November 11, 1918.

136. *Hill Topics*, 1923.

137. *The Toronto Daily Star*, November 11, 1918.

138. *Rosedale Topics*, May 5, 1923.

139. *Toronto's 100 Years*, J.E. Middleton, p. 108.

140. *York Pioneer and Historical Society* - see Annual Report for 1928 for a short account of O.B. Sheppard.

141. *Hill Topics*, January 6, 1923.

142. *The Globe*, August 1910; and information supplied by the present Company.

143. *Hill Topics*, January 21, 1922.

144. Ibid.

145. RECOLLECTIONS of Harry Buse (died 1975), the son of the family that ran the blacksmith and carriage shop for many years on the corner across from Steele's Hotel.

146. *Aurora Banner*, April 1, 1898.

147. *The Globe*, November 30, 1910.

148. *Hill Topics*, December 31, 1921.

149. Ibid, January 6 and July 7, 1923.

150. Ibid, June 23, 1923.

151. Report of the Lieutenant Governor's Committee on Housing Conditions in Toronto, 1934.

152. Ibid.

153. *Rosedale Topics*, February 26 and March 12, 1921.

154. *The Globe*, October 16, 1933.

155. *North Star*, January 3, 1979.

156. *The Globe*, October 16, 1933.

157. Ibid, October 27, 1933.

158. Ibid, October 20, 1933.

159. Ibid, July 22, 1935.

160. *Dominion of the North*, Donald Creighton, p. 514.

161. *The Globe*, June 24, 1938.

162. Ibid, June 25, 1938.

163. Ibid, June 30, 1938.

164. Ibid, June 22, 1938.

165. Ibid, August 1 and 2, 1938.

166. Ibid, August 15, 1938 and August 21, 1939.

167. See the *Globe and Mail*, and the *Toronto Daily Star*, May 22, 23, 1939.

SELECTED
BIBLIOGRAPHY

Adam, G. Mercer. *Toronto, Old and New*. Toronto: The Mail Printing Company, 1891.

Armstrong, Christopher and Nelles, H.V. *The Revenge of the Methodist Bicycle Company*; Sunday Streetcars and Municipal Reform in Toronto, 1888-1897. Toronto: Peter Martin Associates Limited, 1977.

Barry, James P. *Georgian Bay, the Sixth Great Lake*. Toronto: Clarke, Irwin and Company Limited, 1968.

Clark, C.S. *Of Toronto the Good; A Social Study. The Queen City of Canada as it is*. Montreal: The Toronto Publishing Company, 1898.

Cook, James, A., Printer. *North Toronto in Pictures, 1889-1912*. Toronto: 1974.

Davies, Blodwen. *Storied York: Toronto Old and New*. Toronto: The Ryerson Press, 1931.

Fitzgerald, Doris M. *Old Time Thornhill*. Thornhill: 1970.

Gazette Steam Print, Publisher. *Historical Sketch of the Town of Barrie*. Barrie: 1884.

Glazebrook, G.P. de T. *The Story of Toronto*. Toronto: University of Toronto Press, 1971.

Glazebrook, G.P. de T. *A History of Transportation in Canada*. The Carleton Library No. 11. Toronto: McClelland and Stewart Limited, 1964.

Goheen, Peter G. *Victorian Toronto; 1850 to 1900*. Research Paper No. 127. Chicago: University of Chicago Department of Geography, 1970.

Guillet, Edwin C. *Toronto; from Trading Post to Great City*. Toronto: The Ontario Publishing Company Limited, 1934.

Hale, Katherine. *Toronto; Romance of a Great City*. Toronto: Cassell and Company Limited, 1956.

Howard, David James, *True Life Story*. Richmond Hill Public Library, 1972.

Hunter, Andrew F. *A History of Simcoe County, in two parts*. Edition reproduced by the Historical Committee of Simcoe County, 1948.

Jackes, Lyman B. *Tales of North Toronto*, in 2 vols. Reproduced by the North Toronto Business Men's Association, 1948.

Johnson, Rev. Hugh, D.D. *A Merchant Prince. Life of Hon. Senator John Macdonald*. Toronto: William Briggs, 1893.

Johnston, James, M.A. Ph.D. *Aurora; Its Early Beginnings*. Published by the Aurora Centennial Committee, 1963.

Masters, D.C. *The Rise of Toronto; 1850-1890*. Toronto: University of Toronto Press, 1947.

McKenty, Neil. *Mitch Hepburn*. Toronto: McClelland and Stewart Limited, 1967.

Morton, Desmond. *Mayor Howland; The Citizen's Candidate*. Toronto: Hakkert, 1973.

Mulvany, C. Pelham. *Toronto: Past and Present*. Toronto: W.E. Caiger, 1884.

Myers, Jay. *The Great Canadian Road—a history of Yonge Street.* Toronto: Red Rock Publishing Company Limited, 1977.

Rattray, W.J. *The Scot in British North America,* in 4 vols. Toronto: Maclean and Company, 1880.

Robertson, J. Ross. *A Collection of Historical Sketches of the Old Town of York from 1792 until 1833 and of Toronto from 1834 to 1893.* Toronto: Published from the *Toronto Evening Telegram,* 1894.

Robinson, C. Blackett. *History of Toronto and County of York.* Toronto: Publisher, 1885.

Scadding, Henry, D.D. *Toronto of Old,* ed. F.H. Armstrong. Toronto: Oxford University Press, 1966.

Taylor, C.G. *Toronto "Called Back" from 1897 to 1847.* Toronto: William Briggs, 1897.

West, Bruce. *Toronto.* Toronto: Doubleday Canada Limited, 1967.

Miscellaneous: Articles, Pamphlets, Reports.

Aurora Heritage Properties, in 2 vols. Prepared by the Local Architectural Conservation Advisory Committee, 1978.

Berrin, Ralph. 'Henry Blackstone or How Henry Died.' *The York Pioneer,* 1964.

Crawford, M. Gail. 'The Redoubtable Carriage.' *The York Pioneer,* 1975.

Coatsworth, Emerson S. 'The Toronto General Burying Grounds.' *The York Pioneer,* 1971.

Henderson, Elmes. 'Some Notes on a Visit to Penetanguishene and the Georgian Bay in 1856.' Toronto: Ontario Historical Society Papers and Records Vol. XXVII, 1932.

Keys, Norman A., Q.C. 'Yorkville in the Nineties.' *The York Pioneer,* 1964.

Report of the Lieutenant-Governor's Committee on Housing Conditions in Toronto, 1934. Archives of Ontario.

Scadding, Henry, D.D. 'Yonge Street and Dundas Street: The Men After Whom They Were Named.' *The Canadian Journal of Science Literature and History,* Vol. XV, No. VIII, January, 1878.

Scrapbooks of Mary Vallière, Richmond Hill, Ontario, 1982.

Simpson, B. Napier Jr. 'A Walking Tour of Thornhill.' *The York Pioneer,* 1966.

The Port and Harbour of Toronto, 1834-1934. Toronto Harbour Commissioners. Archives of Ontario.

Transit in Toronto, 3rd Edition, 1971. Archives of Ontario.

Village of Bedford Park Walk.' Sponsored by Central Eglinton Historical Society. Metropolitan Library of Toronto, June, 1978.

Wheels of Progress. T.T.C. Story of the development of Toronto and its public transport. Archives of Ontario.

York Pioneer, The (1974). 'A Ceremony and Walk at Holland Landing'.

Yorkville Old Boys and Girls Association; 7th Annual Banquet and At-Home, Tuesday, February 18, 1913. Archives of Ontario.

Atlases/Directories

Brown's Toronto General Directory, 1861. Archives of Ontario.

Charles E. Goad's Atlas. 2nd Edition, 1890. 'Atlas of the City of Toronto and Vicinity.' 3rd Edition, 1910 amended to 1923. Archives of Ontario.

City Directory, 1905. Archives of Ontario.

Hutchinson's Toronto Directory, 1862-63. Archives of Ontario.

Might's Directory, 1895.

Rowsell's City of Toronto and County of York Directory, 1850-1. Archives of Ontario.

Newspaper Sources

Aurora Banner
The Barrie Examiner and Barrie Saturday Morning
The Daily Telegraph
The Evening Globe
The Evening Telegram
The Globe
The Globe Weekly
Hill Topics
The Liberal (Richmond Hill, Ont.)
The Mail
Mail and Empire
The Midland Free Press
The Newmarket Era
The North Toronto Echo
The North Toronto Progress
The Penetanguishene Herald
Rosedale Topics
The Sentinel and Orange and Protestant Advocate
Star Weekly
The Telegram
The Toronto Daily Star
The Toronto World
The Weekly Sun
York Herald

INDEX

By the same author...

THE YONGE STREET STORY 1793-1860

This is the remarkable story of the trail that became the longest street in the world, as officially recognized by *The Guinness Book of Records*. Begun in 1794, Yonge Street was planned by the ambitious Lieutenant Governor John Graves Simcoe as a military route between Lake Ontario and Lake Huron. Anxious to bolster Upper Canada's defences against the new republic to the south, which he heartily loathed, Simcoe had his Queen's Rangers survey and develop the route from Toronto to present-day Holland Landing, and laid out lots for settlement. Even the trusty Rangers, as one surveyor complained in 1799, needed little excuse to down tools and vanish "to carouse upon St. George's day".

Handsomely illustrated with the author's drawings, and painstakingly researched, this book captures the not-so-distant days when muddy Yonge Street was the backbone of pioneer Ontario.

What the reviewers have said:

"Berchem is a literate writer and his prose has a touch of wry humour.... Berchem obviously enjoyed putting *The Yonge Street Story* together and it is enjoyable to read. As befits a naval commander ... his book is what you might expect his ship to be – crisp, in good order, hospitable, and quite dependable." Gordon Dodds in *Quill & Quire*

"F.R. Berchem's *Yonge Street Story* was well received as an enjoyable popular local history when it came out in 1977. As it has stood the test of time well, its reissue during the bicentennial of Canada's most famous street is good news because it is now available to a new generation of history buffs who are sure to enjoy Mr. Berchem's literate and insightful book." Carl Benn, *Toronto Historical Board*

"One of the best pieces of historical writing that I have read in recent years." E.L. Crowther in *Early Canadian Life*

"He writes an excellent narrative ... and he also contributes historically exact and well researched sketches that he has drawn for the book. It just lives and breathes with people." Dean Tudor in *Canadian Book Review Annual*

Published by Natural Heritage/Natural History Inc. • ISBN 1-896-219-13-6 • $19.95